SCENES FROM THE PAST : 45

MANCHESTE
LONDON ROAD
TO
HAYFIELD

VIA REDDISH, BREDBURY, ROMILEY, MARPLE & NEW MILLS

AND INCLUDING THE 'HYDE LOOP'

Manchester London Road, c.1952. Crowds of trainspotters congregate at the south end of the eastern platforms at Manchester London Road. Class C13 4-4-2T No **67425** has just received the signal to vacate the station. In all probability, the engine will be going back to Gorton for servicing as it has been given access to the main line rather than the siding it would use if it were going to reverse back on to another train. To the right of the picture are the steps leading up to the GCR signal box controlling the eastern side of the station. The younger schoolboys, complete with shorts, blazers and long socks contrast strongly with the older boys wearing long trousers. School caps proliferate in those days before designer clothing school uniforms were worn for casual and formal occasions alike. Judging by the shadows, this is late afternoon and the spotters are making a detour on their way home from school. ***Eric Oldham***

IAN R SMITH & GREG FOX

ISBN 1 870119 73 8

DESIGNED BY G K FOX

PRINTED BY THE AMADEUS PRESS, CLECKHEATON

PUBLISHED BY FOXLINE (PUBLICATIONS) LTD

P O BOX 84, BREDBURY. SK6 3YD

Class A5 4-6-2T No **69823** with a Manchester London Road to Hayfield train, approaches Marple North Tunnel shortly after passing Marple Wharf Junction in 1954. The carriages are wooden bodied suburban stock of Gresley design from the LNER. The first five of the A5 Class locomotives were allocated to Gorton with a view to displacing some of the C13/14 locomotives that had already been in service for half a century. The train was typical of those which were provided for the Hayfield and Macclesfield line services prior to the introduction of diesel multiple units. ***Eric Oldham***

CONTENTS

Manchester (London Road) to Hayfield

Hayfield, 1954. Signalling and locomotive livery apart, this view of a bunker first departure by one of the Great Central built 4-4-2 tank engines typified generations of train departures from the Derbyshire terminus of Hayfield. Class C14 No **67447** leaves with a working for Manchester London Road. Note the stored carriages both left of the train and adjacent to the station. ***C H A Townley***

Foreword

For just over a century, trains climbed from the centre of Manchester to the Derbyshire village of Hayfield. They carried generations of hikers and commuters to towns and villages where clean air and steep hills bore little resemblance to the industrial and commercial surroundings of Lancashire. On the short journey of less than an hour, the passenger would cross foaming rivers on high viaducts, see beautiful woodlands and get glimpses of Derbyshire's Peak District.

As throngs of eager passengers surged past the buffers at Hayfield and looked ahead, there, beyond the pretty village, were the brooding shoulders of the fells that provided so much incentive and challenge; the way to Kinder Scout. It was on the moors of Kinder that the Ramblers Association achieved a phenomenal public relations coup in the 1920s when train-loads of passengers joined in the mass trespass that eventually allowed free pedestrian access to the moors of the Dark Peak. The 'Hayfield' line in one sense was pivotal in opening up the possibilities of the Peak District to the working classes of Manchester.

On 5th January 1970, the line was axed between New Mills and Hayfield. This saw the closure of Hayfield and Birch Vale Stations. It was a bad day for passenger routes in the area for the line from Rose Hill (Marple) to Macclesfield Central, and services on the line from Manchester Piccadilly to Sheffield Victoria (the Woodhead Line) were curtailed on the same date. The routes, both via Hyde and Reddish, serving the Manchester Piccadilly to Hayfield services had been proposed for closure but, when push came to shove, it was the final section from New Mills to Hayfield that was attacked. Political expediency won.

In retrospect it can be argued that the loss of the New Mills to Hayfield line was largely unnecessary. The reasons for closure included the cost of infrastructure maintenance. Basically the tunnel at New Mills was considered to be likely to require huge sums to keep it viable. The irony is that, following closure of the through route to Hayfield, that very tunnel became a useful siding for holding trains that had arrived from Manchester. For many years, they went into the tunnel and waited there for the equivalent time taken to have gone to Hayfield and back. At the time of closure it was stated that commuters and hikers would use New Mills Central and then travel by bus to Hayfield. Few ever took up that option.

The route from New Mills Central to Manchester Piccadilly has survived intact. Even the line from Romiley to Hyde North, which appeared in the Beeching proposals as a candidate for closure by being linked with the Macclesfield line, was reprieved without ever having to face a formal closure proposal.

Ian R Smith and G K Fox - January 2003

GENESIS

The line from Manchester London Road (now known as Piccadilly) to Hayfield had its origins in the desire of competing companies to link Manchester with Sheffield. In 1813 a scheme had been put forward to link the two cities by a combination of canals and inclined plane railways. The problem was 'solved' by the completion of the direct line between the two cities using the Woodhead Tunnel to breach the Pennines in 1845. It was owned by the Sheffield, Ashton-under-Lyne & Manchester Railway (SA&MR), a company which had designs on opening up the area to the south and west of its Woodhead route.

In 1843, horse-drawn passenger boat connections were provided with SA&MR trains at Dukinfield Dog Lane (on the Guide Bridge - Stalybridge line) along the Peak Forest and Macclesfield Canals to both Marple and Macclesfield. This service must have been leisurely bearing in mind the flight of sixteen locks at Marple, but it marks the first incursion of railway interests along the route.

It was not long before a railway line up the Goyt Valley through Marple was promoted. The SA&MR, which became part of the Manchester, Sheffield & Lincolnshire railway (MS&LR) in 1847, promoted a line from Hyde Junction via Marple to Whaley Bridge, with a branch to Hayfield. It was intended that the line would then extend to Buxton. This route was authorised in 1846.

The same year saw the SA&MR take over the Ashton, Peak Forest and Macclesfield Canals, increasing their grip on the area. The Peak Forest Tramway was also absorbed at the same time. Work began on the construction of the line from Hyde Junction to Whaley Bridge in 1847.

However, confidence in railway investment fell after the so-called railway mania bubble burst in 1845, and so new works were cut back. The Whaley Bridge branch had reached Hyde when work stopped in 1848. In 1851 powers for constructing the line beyond Hyde lapsed and the rails between Hyde Junction and Hyde were taken up for reuse elsewhere.

Meanwhile the MS&LR suffered an invasion of its territory when the Stockport, Disley and Whaley Bridge Railway (SD&WBR) was authorised in 1854. Nominally independent, the scheme was really a project of the London and North Western Railway. By this means, the LNWR was able to siphon traffic from the Cromford & High Peak Railway from the Peak Forest Canal at Whaley Bridge. Effectively this scuppered the pretensions of the MS&LR for reaching Whaley Bridge and Buxton.

Relations with the LNWR deteriorated over the next few years, and assurances of being a good neighbour were sometimes disregarded by the larger company. This was illustrated by the LNWR arranging the eviction of the MS&LR ticket clerk out of London Road station with his supply of tickets being ejected into the road after him. In spite of such hostility, or maybe because of it, the MS&LR continued to press on towards the Peak District.

CONSTRUCTION FROM HYDE TO COMPSTALL (MARPLE VIADUCT)

In 1858 the Hyde branch had been reopened for passenger traffic from Guide Bridge. That same year, powers were sought to extend the line via Woodley and Romiley to Compstall. The single line opened on 5th August 1862 with the terminus near to Marple Aqueduct. It is believed that the station buildings on the Down (northbound) platforms at Romiley and Woodley date from this time. However, additions to both buildings, the former in the way of the stair hall, changed their appearance.

No illustrations appear to have survived of the terminus at Compstall. Being of a temporary nature, it was probably of wooden construction. From the beginning, Compstall was referred to as Marple in Bradshaw's Guide, although unsuspecting passengers from any of the eight trains each day would have quite a surprise at the distance and terrain to cover on foot.

In 1860, Parliament incredibly passed two Bills offering railway facilities to Hayfield. The Marple, New Mills and Hayfield Junction Railway (MNM&HJR) was backed by the MS&LR. This prompted the LNWR to support a rival, the Disley and Hayfield Railway, as a branch off the nominally independent SD&WBR.

Ultimately, the Disley and Hayfield line was dropped in favour of the Marple line, but not before some earthworks had been constructed in the Sett Valley at Thornsett.

CONSTRUCTION - SOUTH OF COMPSTALL.

Compared to the line from Hyde to Compstall, the section to New Mills presented some fearsome obstacles. The most impressive structure on the line took the railway from its temporary terminus at Compstall across the Goyt Valley. Marple Viaduct (No 30), a structure of 14 spans, carries the line 124 feet (38 metres) above the river on thirteen stone arches, with a large skew girder bridge at the southern end spanning the Peak Forest Canal, giving a total length of 918 feet (280 metres). The canal itself crosses the Goyt Valley by means of a remarkable aqueduct which opened in 1808. Whilst the aqueduct had taken seven years to build, the railway viaduct was completed in only twelve months.

Where the present-day Rose Hill branch joins the main line at the south end of Marple Viaduct there used to be another branch off the main line. Leaving the route just beyond Marple Wharf signal box, and travelling in a southerly direction, it connected the railway with wharves on the Peak Forest Canal. The Wharf branch was built originally to bring materials from the canal to aid the construction of the viaduct. Once in place it was decided that it should remain and so it served a commercial purpose for some years. However, as canal traffic declined so did use of Marple Wharf and the track was lifted around 1900.

The spanning of the Goyt by Marple Viaduct was the beginning of further obstacles in the construction of the line southwards. Immediately having crossed the viaduct and past the junction at Marple Wharf, the line enters a wide cutting before being swallowed by Marple North Tunnel (99yards - 90metres). This short tunnel takes the line under the Peak Forest Canal before it enters the sylvan setting of Brabyns Park and Marple Station. Almost immediately from the south end of the station the line climbs and twists as it holds on to a narrow shelf blasted out of the steep sides of the valley high above the River Goyt. This takes the line through Marple South Tunnel (225 yards - 206 metres), and on to a spectacular shelf with a cutting wall 50 feet (15 metres) high on one side and a sheer drop on the other. Passing under the footbridge known both as Arkwright's Bridge and the Iron Bridge, the line crosses the Goyt again on a viaduct (Goyt Cliff; No 23) of eight openings, with seven stone arches and a span comprising wrought iron girders over the river itself. With the gradient stiffening again to 1 in 100, southbound trains are faced with a continuous climb along the east side of the valley to Strines. Strines station, located on a gentle hillside, was never a busy station. Situated in a somewhat remote spot, its siting was perhaps more suited for the convenience of the railway engineers rather than the communities it purported to serve.

New Mills (later Central) is built on a ledge hewn from the rock whilst a short distance to the south, supporting the railway above the river, is a huge retaining wall. Immediately to the east of this is the junction from which the Hayfield branch diverged from the main line, both routes entering tunnels which carried them beneath the town centre of New Mills.

The line through Marple suffered great delays in its construction as a result of the huge engineering problems that were faced. Although Marple Viaduct was completed by April 1863, trains did not commence public services as far as New Mills until 1st July 1865. Strines opened the following year in 1866.

As originally built, the line was single with platforms on the present day 'Down' (or Manchester) alignment. No goods facilities were provided at first. From the opening, the temporary station at Compstall closed. Eight trains a day were provided from the start by the MS&LR with which company the MNM&HJR was amalgamated on 5th July 1865.

By this time reports were circulating that the LNWR was considering a line from Chapel-en-le-Frith to Sheffield, and that its Hayfield option might be revived. This undoubtedly spurred the MS&LR into pressing on with the line from New Mills to Hayfield.

The Hayfield branch posed no major engineering problems in its route of just over 2¾ miles except for the tunnel under New Mills (Hayfield Tunnel; No 13 - 197yds). Opening to passenger traffic on 1st March 1868, its was built with a double line formation. It was always single except for the first half mile out of New Mills, which initially served as a lie-bye for the branch before being adapted for the needs of the Watford Bridge premises of Messrs Rumney, and a short section on the approach to Hayfield.

POLITICS

Back in Manchester the difficulties with the LNWR continued. Whilst the SA&MR had used a terminus in Travis Street, near to the LNWR terminus, the London Road Station Act of 1859 required the LNWR and MS&LR to cooperate in a joint station with a General Superintendent in overall control. The new London Road station opened in 1866, divided into two separate halves by a large iron railing.

The Midland Railway had tried a number of options to reach Manchester. It had hoped to run trains from Derby to Buxton and on to Manchester via the SD&WBR but found, not unsurprisingly, that the LNWR blocked its moves. The MS&LR line to Hayfield gave the Midland an opportunity of gaining access to Manchester by sharing tracks from New Mills.

EARLY INCREASES IN TRAFFIC

By October 1866 Midland goods trains were using the connection via New Mills, although services were interrupted for a few months by the landslip at Bugsworth (now Buxworth). On 1st February 1867 the Midland began a service from London King's Cross to Manchester London Road via New Mills, Marple and Hyde. Eighteen months later, upon completion of its own London terminus, the Midland trains were diverted to St Pancras.

The through running of trains from the Midland Railway made the doubling of the line a necessity. This was accomplished between New Mills and Hyde Junction in 1866, along with the construction of additional platforms at all stations.

In order that costs as well as benefits might be shared, the MS&LR proposed that the Midland should join it in the formation of a joint operation between New Mills and Hyde Junction.

On 24th June 1869 an Act was passed transferring costs and management to the Sheffield and Midland Joint Committee (S&MJC). It had equal members of board members from each vesting company.

The Midland soon wielded influence in the construction of goods depots at Woodley, Romiley, Marple, Strines and Hayfield in 1870. Later they also appeared at Hyde and Birch Vale. The Midland had its own depot at New Mills and so an S&MJC facility was never built there.

CONNECTIONS

The Manchester and Stockport Railway (M&SR) was a scheme to bring a line from Ashburys to Brinnington Junction on the Cheshire Lines Committee (CLC) route from Godley to Stockport Tiviot Dale. The line was authorised in 1866 with four of the seven directors coming from the MS&LR. However, the MS&LR could see that by adding a connection from Reddish Junction to Romiley it could bring the Midland on board to pay some of the costs. When in 1869 the S&MJC was formed, the Midland agreed to accept the unfinished Manchester and Stockport Railway as part of the joint line.

It was also agreed that a further line should be built, this time connecting Romiley with the CLC at Bredbury Junction. This gave the Midland direct access to Liverpool via the CLC as well as a more direct route into Manchester avoiding the congestion around Guide Bridge.

The 'Marple (or Romiley) Curve' from Bredbury Junction to Romiley Junction opened for goods on 15th February 1875 and for passengers on 1st April. The lines from Ashburys to Romiley, and Brinnington Junction to Reddish Junction were opened on 17th May 1875 for goods, followed by passenger traffic on 2nd August. Intermediate stations were opened at Belle Vue and Bredbury in September 1875, and Reddish in December. Brinnington and Ryder Brow were to follow a century later.

From the beginning a local service was operated by the MS&LR between Manchester London Road and Stockport Tiviot Dale. Some of the Manchester to Hayfield workings were diverted to operate via Reddish instead of Hyde. All Midland main line trains ran via Reddish to Manchester although some Midland stopping services continued to go via Hyde.

The opening of Manchester Central station on 1st July 1880 gave the Midland its opportunity to have its own prestigious terminal in Manchester. From that date the Midland transferred its principal services to Central, trains travelling along the S&MJC between New Mills and Bredbury Junction but then using the route through Stockport Tiviot Dale. Midland stopping services continued to use the two routes to London Road until 1884 when they were all transferred to Central.

NEW FEEDER TRAFFIC

Further traffic was brought to the route by the opening of the Macclesfield, Bollington and Marple Railway (MB&MR) on 2nd August 1869. It left the S&MJC at Marple Wharf Junction by means of a tight curve. In 1871 the line was vested jointly between the North Staffordshire Railway (NSR) and MS&LR, becoming the Macclesfield Committee Railway. Early possibilities of the line forming a new thrust for the MS&LR towards London came to naught when a possible amalgamation between the NSR and MS&LR was deflected by LNWR pressure on the North Stafford company.

Initial train services from the Macclesfield line on to the S&MJC connected Macclesfield and Manchester London Road via Hyde. There were four each way (two on Sundays).

...............................*Continued on page 6*

London Road, 22nd July 1959. Trains for Hayfield commenced their journey from the eastern side of London Road station in Manchester. Before the station was almost completely gutted and rebuilt as Piccadilly, this official British Railways photograph illustrates how things had been in the years leading up to modernisation. It shows the view looking from the former London Midland (LNWR/LMS) side across the concourse to the eastern side. Beyond the Luggage Office in the middle of the picture can be seen the sign for Platforms 1 to 3, from which the Hayfield (and Macclesfield via Rose Hill) trains would depart. To the right, the ticket barriers control access to the platforms whilst passengers, including a group of scouts from the 1st Marple troop, await news of their train. The Special Traffic Notice on the right advises that two relief trains will run to London on Sunday at 5.15 and 5.40 respectively. Within a matter of months, this side of the station would be closed to traffic and a good proportion of the trains for Macclesfield Central/Rose Hill, Marple and Hayfield would commence their journeys from the LM platforms. A far greater number however, started/terminated at Ardwick and Ashburys with bus connections to and from Ducie Street. A time of twenty minutes was allowed for the journey and transfer to/from trains at Ashburys. Local services on the dc electrified lines from Glossop and Hadfield terminated at Ashburys, whilst trains that normally called at Ardwick would start/terminate there. Trains to and from Sheffield Victoria were diverted to either Manchester Victoria or Manchester Central. These arrangements covered the period between 3rd January and 24th April 1960, following which work progressively encroached upon the London Midland platforms, resulting in a greater involvement by Mayfield station. *British Railways/Harry Bedford*

Continued from page 5....

Passenger trains were worked throughout by the MS&LR but goods traffic was in the hands of the NSR, presumably only between Rose Hill and Macclesfield.

Diversionary Route

By the end of the Nineteenth Century traffic using the S&MJC was very heavy. The Midland was offering main line and local passenger trains from the Derby and Sheffield lines. Significant numbers of goods trains were coming from the Midlands, Yorkshire and the Peak District. The MS&LR had its local trains on the Hayfield and Macclesfield routes, as well as the Manchester to Stockport route. Delays, particularly in the Romiley and Guide Bridge areas were frequent.

The Midland found such delays very constrictive and sought ways of avoiding the line from Stockport to Bredbury (a heavily graded route shared with an almost continuous procession of slow-moving goods trains on the CLC route and the S&MJC itself.

A new avoiding line was authorised in 1898 to take Midland trains from New Mills South Junction to Heaton Mersey. A spacious new replacement station was to be built at Chinley, and a sizeable goods marshalling yard at Gowhole. The new line opened throughout on 1st July 1902 and from that time Midland Railway express traffic and many goods trains ceased to use the S&MJC.

The Grouping

On 1st August 1897 the MS&LR became the Great Central Railway (GCR), reflecting the fact that with its London Extension it was no longer a provincial undertaking. In 1922, legislation resulted in the Grouping of the railways into the 'Big Four'. The Midland became part of the London Midland and Scottish Railway (LMSR) whilst the Great Central came under the aegis of the London and North Eastern Railway (LNER). These changes had no obvious effect on the running of the Joint lines. Travel by LNER train did not improve as a result of these changes and in the 1920s there were a number of public complaints about their continued use of archaic six wheeled stock. Mostly these were non-corridor and gas-lit. In contrast the LMSR had inherited the Midland's bogie coaching stock, and reaped the benefit of that company's advanced thinking on passenger comfort.

By 1938, the LNER was running 32 trains a day from Manchester, about half terminating at Marple. This was 25% more than the GCR managed in 1910. The LMSR was offering sixteen trains each way. The difference was that, prior to the turn of the century, the local trains had to fit in with the predominant main line workings of the Midland. By 1938 the local service was much more frequent with more trains in the peak hours.

Between the wars LNER trains were usually hauled by GCR (MS&LR) 2-4-2Ts, although these were gradually replaced by the more powerful GCR 4-4-2Ts of Class C13. LMS trains were mainly hauled by elderly Midland locomotives displaced from front line work by the Compound 4-4-0s.

The infrastructure of the line was little changed during this time except for gradual rationalisation of signalboxes. Oakwood and Goyt Viaduct signal boxes closed in 1933, for example. One major undertaking was the repairs to Goyt Cliff Viaduct between Marple and Strines. The voids between the spandrels of the stone arches had originally been filled with clay. This was replaced over a number of years during the 1930s with concrete.

Manchester London Road, July 1959. Looking in the opposite direction to that on page 6, this scene met passengers leaving the eastern side platforms. On the right is the entrance to the former MSLR/GCR/LNER/ER Refreshment Buffet, a facility duplicated across the service road by the erstwhile LNWR/LMS/LMR hostelry. To the left of Wymans (*later Menzies*), the tender of a Stanier locomotive is just visible.

Second World War

The Second World War resulted in savage cuts to services. From 1st November 1939 the LNER services between Marple and Manchester London Road were reduced from 32 to 20. The LMS through coaches to Manchester Victoria and East Lancashire (detached from LMS expresses at Chinley), were abolished at the outbreak of war. This left a service of nine Up and eight Down local trains operating between Manchester Central and Chinley, some continuing to Sheffield, Buxton or Derby. Another casualty was the Marple to Stockport shuttle service. It appeared that war was an excuse to get rid of uneconomic services for none of those which were axed ever reappeared with the outbreak of peace. Of the 94 trains run daily by the LMS and LNER in 1938, only 61 continued in 1944.

Post-War Recovery and Nationalisation

Following nationalisation of the railways (1st January 1948) the Manchester -Hayfield routes became part of the London Midland Region although the motive power and rolling stock continued to be supplied by Eastern Region authorities. During the first few years following Nationalisation, the ageing C13 Class was supplemented by its marginally younger cousin, the C14. In the early 1950s they were strengthened by the arrival of the Class A5 4-6-2Ts. Gorton shed (39A) was later transferred to London Midland control, becoming 9G, a sub-shed of Longsight.

Recovery after the war was slow. In the early 1950s, pre-Grouping locomotives and rolling stock provided the norm on Hayfield passenger trains. The diet of C13 and C14 4-4-2Ts and A5 4-6-2Ts was unbroken except for the occasional Jll 0-6-0 when there was a crisis. On the Midland services between Romiley and New Mills, 4-4-0s of 2P or 4P (Compound) variety were common. On the goods trains, Gorton provided the motive power (usually a J11 0-6-0) for the locals, although the through trains heading for the Midland route through Chinley had a wide variety of motive power of Midland (2F, 3F and 4F 0-6-0), LNW (7F 0-8-0), LMS (5MT 2-6-0 and 4-6-0, 8F 2-8-0) and WD (2-8-0) origin. Goods trains produced occasional LNER locomotives such as 04 2-8-0s working to Gowhole; and the Macclesfield line would regularly offer an LMS Fowler 2-6-4T on the pick up goods. As the decade progressed the Midland line trains tended to go over to LMS and BR Standard 4-6-0s, although LMS 2-6-0s of both the 2MT and 5MT were not unknown. On occasions the ill-fated Fell diesel locomotive, No 10100, turned up on Derby to Manchester Central workings via Marple. By the end of the decade the BR 9F 2-10-0 was a regular performer on goods trains.

In 1954, the electrification between Manchester and Sheffield via the GCR Woodhead route was inaugurated. Before the war there had been talk of associated electrification to Marple and Hayfield but this was shelved after hostilities ended. It briefly reappeared in connection with the proposed 'Pic-Vic' project across Manchester in the early 1970s but faded along with that scheme. Nevertheless, matters were critical on the Manchester to Hayfield lines. The use of a few BR Mark 1 suburban coaches, along with some later LNER stock of Thompson design, helped to improve passenger comfort, but the locomotives on the front remained the valiant GCR engines, some of which were half a century old.

Dieselisation of Local Passenger Services

In the Spring of 1956, a diesel multiple unit train was advertised for an excursion to the Peak District, picking up passengers at Romiley, Marple and New Mills. The packed Metropolitan Cammell unit formed of three two-car units attracted scores of people who wanted to see such an exciting glimpse of the future.

Dieselisation of local services on the Hayfield line commenced officially on 16th June 1957. This followed a few months of trial running as the Derby Lightweight two car units were gradually introduced on to services prior to the official handover. The units were classified in the Eastern Region E791XX and E796XX number series, reflecting the fact that Gorton and its sub-sheds were still Eastern Region depots.

The first day of diesel trains to Hayfield, a Sunday, saw a huge increase in passengers eager to try out the new trains (especially to sit behind the driver and see the route ahead). So many people took advantage of the beautiful weather and the new trains that the operating authorities realised that they would have major capacity problems when the crowds returned. Accordingly a steam set was prepared, but hauled by a newcomer to the line, Ll Class 2-6-4T No 67781. This, and a few other classmates had been drafted to Gorton from the London King's Cross suburban lines to cope with the heavy rush hour trains that were not suitable for handing over to diesel units. At a single stroke the GCR tank engines were either consigned to the scrap yard or redeployed on less arduous work elsewhere.

Over the next few years train services blossomed on the Hayfield line. In 1938 there had been 48 daily departures from Manchester London Road for the Marple, Hayfield and Macclesfield lines. By 1955 this had declined to 35, but diesels increased the departures to 57. The basic service was hourly on the hour from Manchester via Reddish to Hayfield and an intermediate service on the half hour which turned back at Marple. In addition, the service via Hyde saw services to New Mills, Marple, Rose Hill and Macclesfield. The Midland local trains continued to offer 9 trains a day.

Diesel multiple units of two or four car formations were normally seen at this time. In the peak times these could be extended to six, eight and even ten car sets. However, it was a fact of life that the suburban coaches from the steam era could carry more people in less space. Diesel units were unable to match the seating capacity of eight suburban coaches. So the Ll 2-6-4Ts held sway for a few years, increased in number in 1960-1 by additional locomotives transferred in from Great Eastern suburban lines.

In 1960 the main terminus for the line, Manchester London Road, had a name change to Piccadilly as part of its rebuilding in connection with the London Midland Region Main Line Electrification project. Whilst steam locomotives were frowned upon in the new bright atmosphere of Piccadilly, they still managed to reach the terminus, and the Hayfield line remained one of the bastions of this type of traction.

Nonetheless, with the steady increase in private cars, and better bus services, passenger numbers dropped steadily after the initial surge following introduction of diesel trains. Gradually the number of peak hour services that could not be handled by diesel trains of modest length dropped. By 1965 there was only the 08.00 Hayfield - Manchester (non-stop after Marple) and the 17.20 return (non-stop to Romiley) which remained steam-hauled. The Manchester Division of the London Midland Region had squeezed out its LNER-derived locomotives and consequently Gorton had given up its Ll's, a 1945 design, in favour of the LMS Fowler 2-6-4Ts which had been introduced in 1927 !

By the early 1960s, more of the 'original' Derby Lightweight diesel units had been drafted in, coming from Buxton and Chester. All units were now in the London Midland M79XXX series, reflecting change of regional responsibilities. Further diesel units of the Metropolitan Cammell design were obtained from Newton Heath to complement the original Derby units. Being non-compatible (yellow diamond) with other units (blue square), the units on the Hayfield route tended not to stray elsewhere and it was unusual to see units from other lines make an appearance.

Temporary arrangements, circa 1960; during the modernisation of London Road. ***Anon***

MIDLAND LINE TRAINS

On the Midland line passenger trains by 1960, various 'refugees' from front line express work were making an appearance. These included 'Jubilee' and 'Royal Scot' 4-6-0s. By now the Midland 2P and 4P 4-4-0's had gone. New diesels took over the Derby workings. These were often in the hands of Metro-Vick Co-Bo Type 2 (Class 28) or the early 'Peak' (Class 44) diesel locomotives. Within only a few years, even these locomotives were chased away as BR/Sulzer Type 2 (Class 24 and 25) Bo-Bo diesels took over the Derby workings. Occasionally these would be headed by later 'Peak' (Class 45) locomotives. The Sheffield line trains remained 50% steam-hauled until the end of 1966. At this time Trafford Park LMS built Class 5MT 4-6-0s would operate along with Canklow (Sheffield) LNER/BR B1 Class 4-6-0s. The use of the B1s gave the line a reminder of its LNER antecedents, even though Gorton had long since abandoned Eastern motive power. Darnall (Sheffield) Brush Type 2 diesels (Class 31) began to appear on some Sheffield trains from about 1965.

CLOSURE OF MANCHESTER CENTRAL AND ASSOCIATED LINES

The former LMS/LM service to Manchester Central ended in January 1967 with the closure of the line from Romiley via Stockport Tiviot Dale. From that time the Derby local service was abandoned but the Hope Valley local service from Sheffield operated non-stop over the Manchester Piccadilly to New Mills Central route. The Sheffield local trains were handed over to Eastern Region Derby 'Heavyweight' (later Class 114) diesel multiple units.

In addition to the Hayfield and Macclesfield services, which carried on as before, the Midland route express trains were diverted away from the Cheadle Heath route and forced to travel via Reddish to Manchester Piccadilly. The St Pancras service was, from the beginning of summer timetable in 1967, greatly reduced as a result of the opening of the full Manchester-Euston electrification via Stoke. Instead, most of the former St Pancras services were curtailed and operated by Cravens two-car (later Class 105) diesel multiple units on a semi-fast service to Chinley, Chesterfield and Nottingham or Derby. A daily London St Pancras working continued, almost invariably hauled by a 'Peak' (Class 45).

CLOSURE OF THE HAYFIELD BRANCH

By now the Beeching clouds were gathering over the services from Manchester Piccadilly to Hayfield and Macclesfield. In a seemingly inexplicable move (presumably to achieve partial closure), the various routes were treated on an individual basis when it came to closure proposals. It was proposed that Manchester to Marple via Reddish should not be closed. The route via Hyde appeared in the Beeching Report as one of those for closure. In addition, Marple to Hayfield and Romiley to Macclesfield were to be axed. In the event, there were reprieves. Marple to New Mills was saved, as was Romiley to Rose Hill. The Hyde line never came up for consideration and survived almost by default but the lines from Rose Hill to Macclesfield and New Mills to Hayfield were not so fortunate.

One of the reasons used in the costings to advocate the closure of the few miles from New Mills Central to Hayfield was the need to save maintenance costs on the tunnel to the south of New Mills Central. Once the line closed this same tunnel was used for nearly two decades as a diesel multiple unit stabling point.

The oft-recorded plea that closure to Hayfield would result in hardship to the thousands of walkers trying to reach the Peak District and, in particular, the footpaths leading up Kinder Scout fell on deaf ears. They could, it was contended, catch the New Mills to Hayfield bus service. As that continued on, via Marple to Manchester, and the station was reached by way of a long steep hill at New Mills Central, it is not surprising that few hikers chose to break their journey in New Mills.

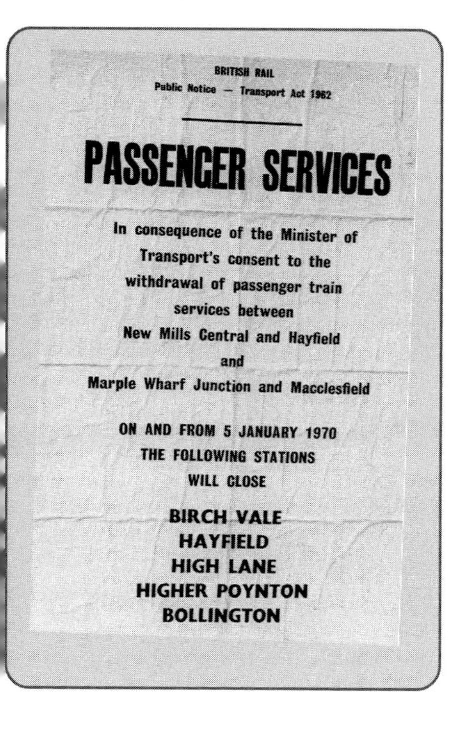
BRITISH RAIL
Public Notice — Transport Act 1962

PASSENGER SERVICES

In consequence of the Minister of Transport's consent to the withdrawal of passenger train services between
New Mills Central and Hayfield
and
Marple Wharf Junction and Macclesfield

ON AND FROM 5 JANUARY 1970
THE FOLLOWING STATIONS
WILL CLOSE

BIRCH VALE
HAYFIELD
HIGH LANE
HIGHER POYNTON
BOLLINGTON

Closure of the Hayfield branch took place as and from 5th January 1970. It was a date locally overshadowed by the loss of the passenger service over the electrified Manchester to Sheffield (Woodhead) route the same day. The Rose Hill to Macclesfield section of line closed at the same time. However, effectively closure was 24 hours earlier as 5th January was a Sunday and the Hayfield (and Macclesfield) branches had no trains on Sundays.

Following closure, the track between New Mills and Hayfield was lifted and the route became overgrown. In 1975 the station buildings were demolished and the site developed as a car park and bus station at the southern end of the Sett Valley Trail, a dedicated walking and cycling route.

IMPROVEMENTS

Involvement of the newly-formed Passenger Transport Authority (PTA) for Greater Manchester, following the Transport Act of 1968, resulted in increased attention being paid to the provision of public transport during the next decade. Hyde to Romiley - the 'Hyde Loop' - was quietly dropped from the list of lines to be closed and gained a PTA subsidy along with the route via Reddish. Two new stations were opened on the Romiley to Reddish line; Brinnington on 12th December 1977 and Ryder Brow on 4th November 1985.

Numerous stations were subsequently 'rationalised'. Marple was completely rebuilt, with only platforms, footbridge (No.27) and signal box remaining from the old order. The 'new' station opened on 28th October 1970. At Belle Vue and Hyde North in particular, the buildings, which had fallen on hard times, were swept away and replaced by shelters. At Reddish North, and Hyde Central, the old buildings were reduced in stature to reflect less important aspirations. New Mills Central, Romiley and Woodley remained as the least altered stations, although facilities on the Up (southbound) platforms at all three suffered accordingly. The order of the day came in the form of 'bus' type shelters, although Romiley retained its buildings and canopy albeit much reduced in length. Strines became an unstaffed halt from 10th September 1973. All stations were electrically lit by 1975, Woodley being the last to give up its gas lights.

LOCAL GOODS FACILITIES WITHDRAWN

Local goods facilities were withdrawn progressively from the mid-1960s. One time important goods yards at Bredbury and Hyde lasted longer than the smaller yards such as Strines (August 1963) and Marple (5th October 1964) but by the beginning of the 1970s all that remained was the facility, albeit private, at Bredbury which catered for the steel products of nearby James Mills. General merchandise was concentrated at New Mills East but this too had closed by 1968. Domestic coal traffic was concentrated at Woodley but even this ceased in 1972. The route also witnessed the national decline in rail-borne goods, so that by 1975 the once frequent flow of freight trains was limited to irregular but scheduled limestone hopper trains travelling between Peak Forest and distribution depots in the Manchester area.

SIGNALLING MODERNISATION

Signalling along the route has been concentrated at Romiley Junction and New Mills. Track circuit block signalling, abolishing manual signalboxes and semaphore signalling was introduced between Ashburys and Romiley in 1973, securing the closures of boxes at Bredbury, Reddish Junction and Belle Vue. Earlier rationalisation had seen closure of the signal boxes at Lingard Lane (1966), Reddish North (1964) and Belle Vue Engine Shed (1965). The Romiley to New Mills resignalling scheme came into effect on 27th July 1980, sweeping away the signal boxes at Marple Wharf Junction, Marple, Strines and New Mills Goods Junction.

SERVICE FLUCTUATIONS SINCE 1970

Other changes on the line which resulted from the closure of the New Mills - Hayfield and Rose Hill - Macclesfield sections of line were connected with the route via Hyde. In the main, the trains from New Mills and Marple now travelled to Manchester via Reddish whereas those from Rose Hill went via Hyde. In fact the Rose Hill service was increased to an unprecedented hourly service.

The fast trains to Nottingham and Derby did not last long. They were axed with the closure of the Peak Forest to Matlock section of the former Midland route through the Peak District on 1st July 1968. However, the closure of the former Great Central route via Woodhead (5th January 1970) brought fast trains between Sheffield and Manchester back on to the line. An hourly service between the two cities was offered, initially using conventional diesel multiple units BRC&W (Class 110) 'Calder Valley' and Metro-Cammell (Class 101) sets. These were replaced by Swindon built Class 'hybrid' 123/124 diesel multiple units. The poor riding qualities and indifferent mechanical performance of these units, especially when compared to the performance of the electric expresses they had replaced, resulted in much adverse comment and so they, in turn, were replaced by elderly Class 31 locomotives hauling short trains of BR Mark 2 carriages.

The slower nature of the route between New Mills and Manchester, combined with the desire to serve Stockport, resulted in the opening of the Hazel Grove "Chord" on 12th May 1986. From that date all fast trains returned to the Midland main line from New Mills South Junction.

Loss of the Manchester - Sheffield express trains resulted in services settling down to being purely local in character, with diesel units stopping at most stations through the day. The Manchester - New Mills Central service was combined with the Sheffield Midland to New Mills Central stopping service. Approximately every other train from Manchester that reached New Mills Central continued on to Sheffield, calling at all stations.

In 1977, Marple had 44 daily trains from Manchester and 42 to Manchester. By 1998, following privatisation of the railways, local passenger train services were operated by First North Western (FNW). This had seen a reduction of trains reaching Marple to 39 from Manchester and 32 to Manchester.

One tradition of the Hayfield line, even after truncation, lives on. Cascaded trains which have seen better days on other areas seem to gravitate to the route. The new millenium saw the continuation of services provided by Metropolitan Cammell diesel multiple units (Class 101) of a design dating back to 1956. By 2003, the line was one of the last in the country to use the old-style diesel units, euphemistically termed 'Heritage Units', although they occasionally substituted elsewhere for services suffering a stock shortage. In order to keep seven units available, various vehicles were brought in as they were discarded by other depots. This resulted in the incongruous sight of orange-liveried Class 101 units bearing Strathclyde PTE insignia.

An innovative move for the summer 2000 timetable had seen the introduction of an hourly 'express' service from Marple to Manchester, inclusive of a stop at Romiley, the whole journey time being sixteen minutes. Despite regular and ongoing reports concerning their future, the 101s continued to operate throughout 2002, entering 2003 with expectations of another twelve months of employment, primarily sharing the Marple/ Rose Hill diagrams with second generation units such as the Class 142 'Pacer', and supplemented by Class 150 and 156 units. Freight trains powered by Classes 60 and 66 locomotives, belonging to English Welsh & Scottish Railways and Freightliner Heavyhaul, marginally increased the number of limestone trains using the line.

MANCHESTER TO HAYFIELD - A BRIEF ROUTE DESCRIPTION

Imagine a journey in 1961 sitting in the compartment behind the Driver of one of the distinctive original Derby Lightweight diesel multiple units. Modernisation of the old London Road Station, as part of the British Railways Main Line Electrification scheme, is under way. The three eastern side platforms have disappeared to be replaced by platforms 1 to 4. So, having paid 3/10d (19p) for a Cheap Day Return (to Hayfield) at the temporary ticket office, we can sit back for approximately three-quarters of an hour for the 15½ mile journey.

Given the 'right-away', the underfloor mounted engines burst into life as the twin exhausts reverberate throatily within the confines of the train shed. The rapid acceleration along the platform is interrupted by a gear change as we emerge into daylight beneath an umbrella of overhead catenary. Ducie Street goods yard sidings fill the left hand side of the station for a short distance before the parapet walls of the viaduct above North Western Street converge to take us the short distance towards Ardwick. Sharing the viaduct with several other running lines, namely those of the western (London Midland) from Stockport and the 'Styal' line, a 'diamond' crossing comes into view shortly before Ardwick which enables movements to and from the 'Midland Curve', a useful link with north Manchester locations via Philips Park. Meanwhile, the elevated views across the rooftops of Ancoats (left) and Ardwick (right) highlight the inner city dwellings that will be swept away within the next decade. A reduction in speed ensues as we move to the left, away from the Crewe lines, adhering to the 35mph restriction on the curve through the platforms of **Ardwick** station. The busy sidings above Ardwick West Goods appear on the left and will continue alongside for some distance as a 1 in 173 gradient is encountered as far as Ashburys West Junction, where the former Midland lines from Midland Junction, Ancoats and Ashton Road converge from the left. Also away to the left are more sidings, this time those of Ardwick East, one time site of the Ashburys Carriage Works. We ease alongside the island platform at Ashburys (for Belle Vue) and note the increasing presence of large factories that proliferate in the eastern districts of Manchester. Of the heavy industries, Crossley Brothers, again to our left, is one of the more notable. The goods lines to our left are perpetually busy, particularly with the transfer of freight between Ashburys Sidings and Ashburys, much of it wagonload in need of shunting. The coaling plant serving Gorton also stands out in the distance beyond Ashburys Sidings, although the presence of overhead electric equipment affects the overall view. It is likely our path towards the branch junction (Ashburys East) will be delayed by the passage of one of the green emu's on the Glossop/Hadfield service. However, after a brief acceleration from the station and past the signal box, we swing right at a maximum 15mph to take 'the (Reddish) branch', and get a view of the defunct Belle Vue Engine Shed on the left of the line. To the right is the impressive outline of *The Church and Monastery of St Francis of Assisi* in Gorton Lane. Passing beneath Gorton Lane (No.1), a shallow cutting of approximately half a mile in length is traversed as far as two closely sited bridges (No2; Cambert Lane) and (No.3; Hyde Road), announcing the approach to **Belle Vue** station, 2½ miles and seven minutes into our journey. This impressive station, with its long platforms, was built from the outset to accommodate the extra traffic generated by the nearby Zoological Gardens and later, Amusement Park. The station buildings are at the Reddish end of the platforms, and as the vacuum brakes are applied, a series of short intermittent 'hissing' sounds are heard from the drivers compartment as the train is brought to a halt. Ahead of us to the right is a small goods yard serving mainly local coal merchants. It is not unusual to see a WD 'Austerity 2-8-0 in the Up Lie-bye siding to the left., taking time out from shunting the yard. There is a slight adverse gradient as we leave the station behind, quickly passing beneath Glencastle Road (No. 7). A long sweeping curve now points us in a south-easterly direction and the line will remain straight for the next one and a quarter miles. On beneath Levenshulme Road (No. 8) - *Ryder Brow station would later be located at this point* - we gather speed, passing a succession of closely spaced overbridges. Wayland Road (No. 9) was rebuilt in 1953 as a footbridge using the original girders. Then follows an intersection bridge (No. 10), which carries the Fairfield to Chorlton line. Occasionally, trains will make an unadvertised stop for staff 'alighting' for the nearby Reddish Electric Traction Depot. Manchester's water supply has crossed the railway system many times on its route from the Lake District, and as we approach Reddish, we will pass beneath the Thirlmere Aqueduct (No. 10A), a large lattice structure built on the skew. The Stockport branch of the Ashton Canal passes overhead a few moments later (No. 11; *demolished in 1965*) before a gentle application of the brakes rings about a speed reduction to pass beneath iorton Road (No. 12) and alongside the latforms of **Reddish North** ($3\frac{3}{4}$ miles). 'he cutting we have travelled along since Belle Vue widens out here on the right to ccommodate the station approach, main uildings and goods yard. The gradient vhich has helped aid our deceleration on the pproach to Reddish acts as something of a indrance on our departure. However, the in 108 climb will end after a few hundred ards as we reach the the 'summit' of the Reddish Branch just beyond Windmill Lane No. 16). The line runs beneath the Heaton Norris to Guide Bridge line (No. 17) at a oint where a junction with that line once erved the long abandoned Denton Colliery. Our train now gathers speed down the 1 in 10 gradient on to a high embankment, and n leaving the Manchester suburbs, we ccelerate into Reddish Vale, crossing the alley of the river Tame on the sixteen arch iaduct (No. 18). To the left in the distance the town of Denton with views beyond of ne Pennine slopes around Saddleworth. To ne right, the river meanders through eddish Vale on a course that will end in tockport where it will merge with the aters of the Goyt to become the River Aersey. The governing line speed of 50mph as a somewhat restraining effect as we eave the viaduct at Reddish Junction, needng to maintain momentum because of the brupt reversal of gradient to 1 in 70 for the tart of a one and a half mile climb. At Reddish Junction, the Brinnington (or Portwood) branch leaves the main line to ne right of the signal box before skirting the astern slopes of Reddish Vale on its way to Brinnington Junction and subsequently tockport Tiviot Dale. Entering a deep cutting vhich bisects Stockport's burgeoning Brinnington housing estate, are two overridges with 'flying' arches which spring off ne embankments sides. *The second of hese, The Link (No. 72) will eventually verlook the site of Brinnington Station, pened in 1977.* With a need to maintain peed and all 150 bhp of the AEC engines in emand, the subsequent vibration and noise rom alloy fittings, such as the luggage racks nd window frames, of these diesel units is omething of an irritation. Lingard Lane Colliery Sidings signal box to the right is a eminder of the district's coal producing past. The box is on the opposite side of the line from vhere the last of the Bredbury 'pits' was ocated, a site nowadays more recognisable by ne huge truss bridge that crosses the M60 Aotorway.

The cutting has now given way to an embankment that will stay with us to all the way to Bredbury. On both sides of the railway there are numerous water filled pits caused by clay extraction when brick making played an important part in the industry of the area. A legacy of this is to be found in Manchester where Bredbury bricks are known to have graced many buildings, particularly in the Whitworth Street area. However, Jacksons (*occupying the site later developed for waste disposal)* are by now the only remaining brick manufacturers, their main site coming into view on the left as we cross Ashton Road (No. 69). An easing of gradient to 1 in 130 enables a quieter ride, the elevated view once again enabling us to enjoy the rural landscape that unfolds before us as we head due south east. The hillside forming Werneth Low spreads itself across the left with the spire of Gee Cross (Hyde) Church prominent. However, the huge water filled clay pit to the left, with the diminutive narrow gauge trains scurrying round the perimeter, dominates the foreground. Over on the distant right, woodland bordering the River Goyt outlines the location of Stockport's Woodbank Park and the district of Offerton. More scarred land borders the railway to the right, although in this instance due a military activity, crew training and testing for tanks and other tracked vehicles. Bredbury Viaduct (No. 67) is crossed as another change in gradient occurs, this time a slight fall as far as Bredbury station, some three hundred or so yards away. The viaduct was constructed to enable the Reddish line to cross both a colliery tramway and the Stockport to Woodley section of the Cheshire Lines (CLC) and the signal box serving Bredbury Junction can be seen in the cutting to the right *(later the site of Bredbury Stone Terminal).* The districts of Woodley (left) and Bredbury border Stockport Road (No. 64) on its east to west route as we roll into **Bredbury** ($6\frac{1}{2}$ miles). Located at the end of one long embankment, it immediately finds itself some thirty or so feet above another, this time created by the converging Bredbury Junction to Romiley Junction line on the right. With the exception of the Station Master's House, the station consists of piled wooden buildings due to its siting on the embankment. Bredbury station has long been at the centre of local industry with factories in close proximity surrounding the site. Most notable are the Bredbury Steelworks of the Exors of James Mills which occupy the land to the far right bordering the railway. The long single storey building to the left of the goods yard was formerly occupied by the Co-operative Laundry. Latterly, it has housed Messrs R K Saxtons, manufacturer of steel pressure vessels, and Redferns (Rubber products). The small goods yard to the left is a 'round the clock' operation *..continued on page 12*

From the new footbridge looking towards the buffers, the new order at Piccadilly. In Platform 6 is a Birmingham RC&W 3-car dmu with the 10.50am to Stoke(FSO), Stafford(FSX). Waiting to leave Platform 3 is a Derby Lightweight set on the 11.00am to Hayfield via Belle Vue. The EMU alongside Platform 2 is the 11.15am to Hadfield. Platform 1 hosts the 11.10am to Sheffield Victoria. ***(BR/LMR)***

continued from page 11......to service the needs of the 'Mills traffic although local coal merchants have stacking and loading facilities. The entrance is on Redhouse Lane, the bridge (No. 63) of which marks the start of a 1 in 93 climb towards Romiley. Passing beneath Redhouse Lane, high red bricked walls to the left distinguish the Hayfield Mills, Bredbury base of Crown, the wallpaper manufacturers. The steep gradient of the 'bottom' line from Bredbury Junction necessitated substantial earthworks and this is no more evident than at this location as we approach Bredbury Tunnel (No. 62). The 'top' line too possesses a steep rock face above and to the left as we enter the 160 yard bore, the engine sounds being amplified during the short confinement. The steep rocky cutting falls away rapidly on leaving the tunnel, transferring the line on to a high embankment created to carry the railway above the Peak Forest Canal, some fifty feet below. The wooded slopes of Werneth Low appear on the left, the natural floor of the 'valley' having long been occupied by the canal and the impressive man made embankment built in 1861 to extend the railway from Hyde through to Marple. With our line still taking a south easterly path, views start to emerge on the right of the hills above Alderley Edge and Lyme Park which mark the eastern edges of the 'Cheshire Plain'. The approach to Quarry Road bridge (No. 60) initiates a speed check as we move towards the junction and its 25mph restriction. The lines from Hyde (left), and Bredbury Junction (right), converge with an immediate easing of gradient to 1 in 237 on which the station is located. According to the 1959 Passenger timetable, **Romiley** station (7½ miles), is served by no less than seventy trains from the Manchester stations of London Road and Central during the week, the twenty two minutes (all stations except Ardwick) via Reddish comparing favourably with the 32/37 via Hyde and 35/41 via Stockport. The station, situated in the centre of the village, enjoys views to the west and south by virtue of its elevated position. Werneth Low again presides to our left, the grassy slopes diminishing as housing development moves apace. Ahead are the hills of the Peak District, the mass of Kinder beginning to show its presence. We leave Romiley behind, with views across the rooftops, and quickly accelerate downhill on the 1 in 150 gradient, the long established Oakwood Mills of the Textile Paper Tube Co. appearing on the right. The open aspect of the landscape will temporarily vanish from view as we pass beneath Oakwood bridge (No. 31) into a short deep cutting that once housed Oakwood signal box. Romiley's Cherry Tree Estate appears on the hillside to the left, together with a skeletal concrete frame locally known as the 'Giants Table'. The Peak Forest Canal returns into view on our right after wandering around Romiley, whilst gentle reverse curves of 34 and 84 chains respectively set up a straight run towards Marple Wharf Junction. With the permissible line speed having been increased to 60mph since Romiley, the driver of the unit has to gauge its momentum in readiness for Marple Wharf Junction where a restriction of 50mph will apply when crossing the junction. Meanwhile, we will emerge from the cutting on to Marple Viaduct (No. 30) the sides of the valley falling away rapidly to the river Goyt below. The imposing presence on the right of Outram's magnificent aqueduct almost demands one's attention whilst over to the left in the distance lies the village of Compstall and the valley of the Etherow. Despite the cautionary brake application, we speed towards the junction, across the Peak Forest Canal and past the signal box, sparing a moment to see the acutely curved Macclesfield line quickly vanish from sight up the deep cutting towards Rose Hill. In a matter of moments our train, having hurried downhill from Romiley, will pass beneath the canal by way of Marple North Tunnel (No.29) and enjoy the wooded surroundings which also help locate Brabyns Park over to our left. The gentle curve that will shortly carry us due south is interrupted as we pass beneath Hudson's bridge (No. 28) and enter **Marple** station (9¼ miles) on the level. The site is efficiently located in the hillside with stone retaining walls which enable a station comprising four platforms to be accommodated. Unfortunately however, this resulted in a somewhat of a cramped goods facility. The frequency of trains and variety of destinations has always given Marple an advantage over its Rose Hill neighbour. Even its location to the east of the district, coupled with the daunting prospect of Brabyns Brow, has done nothing to dissuade potential passengers. Twenty four minutes into our journey, the profile of Brabyns Brow (No. 26) bridge 'frames' our view forward as the engines strain at the start of a 1 in 100 gradient, governed by a 45mph speed restriction over the twenty-six and eighteen-chain radius curves on the ascent towards Marple South Tunnel. The line at this point follows a shallow cutting engineered into a hillside which falls away to the Goyt, behind the wooded area to the left. We soon enter Marple South Tunnel (No. 25), its curvature and darkness temporarily cutting out the light ahead. Above the tunnel, Faywood Drive has now crossed over to the eastern side to become Lakes Road and will appear on our left beyond the high retaining wall at the south end of the tunnel. For the next three miles we will closely follow the course of the Goyt, somewhat precariously at first. A landslide above Bottoms Bridge shortly before Christmas 1893 resulted in closure of the line. It reopened to traffic within two days, the Up line being propped by timber whilst a permanent solution in the form of a stone retaining wall was designed and constructed. The historic 'Roman Lakes' are visible to the left in the valley below as our train approaches Goyt Cliff Viaduct (No. 23). The alignment of the railway follows a gentle south easterly curve to cross the river on this high structure, effectively changing from one side of the valley to the other adjacent to the slopes of Strawberry Hill. A level and straight stretch of line now beckons as Windybottom Wood appears to our left, Cobden Edge also announcing its presence. The valley has opened up again and as we follow the high ground to the left of the river, the Marple to New Mills road claims the opposite side as it threads its way through Strines. The tall chimney that highlights the position of Strines Printworks comes into view on the right and as we pass milepost 175¼ we get a reminder that there is still more than four miles of climbing to do, 1 in 100 at first for a half mile, easing slightly to 1 in 114 as we enter **Strines** station (11¼ miles). High above the village, with an attractive mixture of stone and wooden buildings, the station nestles in a shallow cutting on the hillside. Station Road falls away quite steeply past Strines Print Works before winding its way across the floor of the valley to meet up with Strines Road. A signal from the station staff to the guard results in a growl from the underfloor engines as our Driver acts to engage the unit's gears. Strines is not easiest of places for a train to start from and once again the vibration emanating from the engines causes the alloy components to shake and rattle. The small goods yard on the right has a facing connection to the Down line and with the signal box to our left we leave the station behind with a straight run ahead. However, acceleration does not prove difficult and within minutes we change direction with a gradual (thirty-six chain radius) left hand curve to head due east. The Marple to New Mills road has also changed direction and climbs rapidly to cross over the railway at Hague Bar (No. 16). The road will now accompany the line, albeit at a higher level, with the valley noticably becoming wider and shallower on the approach to New Mills. Across the valley from Hague Bar, the A6 trunk road from Disley has appeared from behind Bowaters factory towards Newtown. The clusters of small dwellings however are soon overshadowed by the dominating presence of the much enlarged Brunswick Mills home of Matlow Brothers *(Swizzels Matlow),* sweet manufacturers of such renowned items as 'Love Hearts', 'Refreshers', etc., Our route ahead is set by long sweeping reverse curves which mark the site, some 400 yards to the west of New Mills Central station, of a collision in 1960 involving freight and passenger trains. **New Mills Central** (12½ miles) is arrived at where road and railway challenge for space above the waters of the Goyt. The railway is spectacularly cut into the hillside with a rock face behind the Up platform. The main station buildings opposite are perched on land which falls away at the rear to the river below. Known locally as the Torrs, the area typifies the town of New Mills with its rocky outcrops. The route ahead still climbs significantly as we accelerate away from the station, firstly beneath a steel lattice footbridge (No. 14A) and then Station Road (No. 14). With New Mills Junction signal box almost abutting the bridge to the right, the rock face on the left becomes higher as the entrance to Hayfield Tunnel (Br. 13) comes into view. To the right is New Mills Tunnel (No. 132), which takes the 'Old' route towards New Mills South Junction and the Midland main line. Both lines pass beneath the town centre, situated high above, subsequently emerging to pass over bridges crossing the River Sett. We emerge into the gorge below Torrs Top, cross the river (No. 12) and pass beneath Hyde Bank Road (No. 11). Our progress is now checked as New Mills Tunnel End signal box appears on the right. With the train reduced to walking pace - a restriction of 4mph is enforcible - the 'token' is collected by the driver from the signalman to enable entry to the single line section. With engines whirring again, the 1 in 78 gradient is tackled, the straight line ahead taking us through this pocket of industry that sits astride the river. Although our train has entered a single line section, the formation carries another line which will continue for a short distance on our left as far as Watford Bridge. Historically, the Sett Valley is connected with the spinning and weaving of cloth. The fast running waters of the river encouraged the development of allied industries resulting in the building of mills as the traditional cottage industry declined. An expanding New Mills is evident with the houses of the Highfield estate covering the hillside to our right. The Sett Valley now opens out, the railway taking a north easterly sweep (52 chain radius, increasing to 132) to cross High Hill Road on a large skew bridge (No. 4), the village of Thornsett appearing on our left. The undulating slopes behind the village which ultimately ascend to Lantern Pike form an inspiring backdrop, whilst to the right, a short man made embankment marks the route of the Disley & Hayfield Railway Company's abortive scheme. Land was acquired between here and Hayfield but the rights to build were never taken up. Thornsett Works appears on the left as we pass over Wyld's *(sic)* - or Garrison - Crossing. River, roads and rail now converge immediately west of **Birch Vale** station (14½ miles), which is reached across a large skew built girder bridge (Station Road; No.1). This single platform station is located above Birch Vale Print Works (Calico) on the southern slope of the valley. The communties served are widespread, with both farming and nearby mills making use of the small goods yard to our right. With less than a mile to go, the gradient now eases to 1 in 119 as long sweeping reverse curves points us due east. To the left, the site of the one time Swallowhouse Mills rests beneath the slopes of Lantern Pike, whilst the road from Glossop (A624) descends from Little Hayfield towards the village of Hayfield itself. Slacks Crossing, controlled by a ground frame, puts us within sight of **Hayfield** station (15½ miles). There are two parallel lines here although that to the left serves as a siding for both the occasional storage of carriages and access to Woods Print Works (Calico). The appearance of the station signal box on the right shortly before Woods Crossing requires a brake application to slow down in order for the signalman to collect the single line token from our Driver. Once over the crossing, our train will enter a level section of line that takes us alongside the station platform, stopping just short of the buffers. The goods yard, partially hidden to our left, is the largest we have seen since Bredbury, indicative of the volume of traffic once handled. After a journey time lasting forty minutes, we are on the fringes of the 'Dark Peak'.

Hayfield, c.1963. These Derby Lightweights had provided a much needed boost to the travelling public since their introduction in 1957. The general all-round views provided by the open seating arrangement, in particular those that could be enjoyed from behind the driver, proved popular with the leisure and tourist element. However, from an operating point of view, the Motor/Trailer combination of the Twin units ultimately proved their undoing on these steeply graded routes on the fringe of the Peak District. ***G K Fox***

MANCHESTER (LONDON ROAD) TO ASHBURYS

Travel into and out of Manchester for users of the trains on the Hayfield and Macclesfield Central lines had remained the same for a half a century or more. It was the 1960s which really changed the face of the railways serving the public of the south eastern suburban areas and the pictures shown on this and the opposing page are intended to give a rapid insight into the scenes that bridged a forty year period.

THE 1930s

(Above) Manchester London Road, 1937. Here we have a view of London Road approach at the height of preparations for the 1937 Coronation of King George V1 and Queen Elizabeth. There would be little change, save for the 1948 nationalisation which resulted in new signage brought about by the formation of British Railways, until the modernisation of 1958-60, when the station was re-named Piccadilly. The left hand, or eastern, side of the station served the three platforms A,B&C of the LNER whilst the major user, the LMS, occupied the lion's share to the right.

(Right-lower) This October 1946 view of Great Central built 4-4-2T, LNER Class C13 No **7424** typifies the type of motive power that had so reliably served the travelling public for the best part of fifty years and would continue to do so for the next decade.

H C Casserley

THE 1940s

THE 1950s

London Road, 30th May 1953. Once again we see a loyal friend in the form of Class C13 4-4-2T No **67403** departing with a train for Hayfield. Apart from the livery change to British Railways identity and the long wheelbase van to the right, the scene has a decidedly Edwardian period feel about it. The train shed on this side dated from 1866 (extended on the south side 1882) and would retain its overall features for almost a hundred years. Even the reconstructions of 1958-60 and late 1990s retained the massive skeletal frame of the train shed whilst all beneath changed almost beyond recognition. ***J F Oxley/M Hartley***

THE 1960s

(Right-centre) London Road, 14th May 1960. The upheaval that had engulfed the station for over two years was drawing to a close although the work required to create the new 'Piccadilly' would carry on for some months as the finishing touches were applied. The area on the 'eastern' side that contained platforms A,B&C had been transformed to become the new platforms 1 to 4, an arrangement that exists to this day. Fowler 2-6-4T No **42373** has brought empty stock into platform 1 in readiness for an electric locomotive to take the train forward to Sheffield. Hadfield electric stock is to be seen alongside platform 4.

H D Bowtell, copyright MLS

London Road, c.1962. The 'new order' had been around since 1957 when DMU services were introduced on the Hayfield and Macclesfield Central services. The distinctive profile of the original 'Derby Lightweight' units can be seen here on a Marple bound train. A yellow panel has by now replaced the 'whiskers' that were first applied across the fronts of the units. The first vehicle is Motor Brake Second **M79143** and was 'twinned' with another motorised unit to cater for the gradients encountered on the routes serving the Peak District. The units themselves had a very short life, this particular vehicle being withdrawn in 1967. The extensive sidings serving Ducie Street Goods are very much in evidence to the right but these would also be redundant from 1967. ***A H Bryant***

(Above) Introduced in 1954 to the Hayfield and Macclesfield line services, this A5 Class 4-6-2T No **69829** makes its way along the last few yards of the journey into London Road. Note the timbered gable ends of Ancoats Goods depot to the left of the locomotive coal bunker. ***Graham Whitehead***

(Centre) On Saturdays, Macclesfield line trains frequently used J11 0-6-0 locomotives instead of their normal weekday tank engines, allowing them to be serviced. In August 1954, presumably on a Saturday, a J11 is seen leaving London Road with a Macclesfield (Central) train. The first two coaches, like the locomotive, are of Great Central Railway origin. The two lines on the eastern side of the viaduct were electrified as part of the Manchester, Sheffield and Wath electrification scheme and these are clearly illustrated here by the presence of the huge cantilevered structures which were anchored to the viaduct walls in North Western Street. They were replaced when the London Midland Main Line Electrification scheme saw extension of the overhead system from Crewe. ***Norman Harrop***

(Right - lower) To both travel behind and experience these venerable machines at first hand leads one to believe that this inbound train from Hayfield, GCR built 4-4-2T No **67437**, visibly rattled its way between Ardwick and London Road. In August 1954 the electrification equipment was still comparatively new which is more than can be said for the locomotive which appears to have a buckled running plate. ***Norman Harrop***

Striding away from Manchester London Road, C13 4-4-2T No **67431** heads for Hayfield in August 1954. The eastern side, although electrified, is still controlled by lower quadrant signals of GC vintage. The carriages behind the engine comprise a Thompson articulated suburban set of late LNER design and were a feature of the services at this time.

ARDWICK

(Right - centre) Ardwick station is just one mile along the line from the terminus in Manchester. It has always chiefly been used by people from the nearby industrial concerns and hence mainly in peak times. However, the nearby Manchester Hippodrome (formerly the *Ardwick Empire)* generated modest amounts of business during matinee and evening performances, although the poorly lit approach to the station along Blind Lane did not help. To the south east of the station were extensive carriage sidings for the Eastern side trains. In March 1954 a C13 4-4-2T No **67438** eases a train of empty carriages out of the sidings on to the southbound track, before crossing over and taking the train into London Road. Judging from the fact that the train is made up of non-corridor suburban stock (the first coach is an LNER Gresley-design half brake) it is likely that this stock would be used for a Hayfield line train. The footbridge at Ardwick has always provided station users with a somewhat daunting climb since the structure was raised to accommodate the overhead electrification equipment. Following the remodelling of 1988, which saw the removal of a very low Up platform, the island platform - which formerly served Down trains - took on a new role. This meant of course that **all** intending passengers had to make their way over several flights of stairs and pathways to reach the platforms.

(Right - lower) March 1954 in the carriage sidings at Ardwick, Class A5 4-6-2T No **69810** has just brought in the empty stock of a train that terminated at Manchester London Road. The pleasing lines of the GCR built coaches combine with the locomotive to exude a pre-Grouping atmosphere over thirty years after the end of the Great Central. Only the electrification catenaries and wires show the advance in years.
This page:all: ***Norman Harrop***

Ashburys for Belle Vue, so the 'running in' board proclaims, was one of four stations in the area serving the needs of the nearby Belle Vue Zoo and Amusement Park; the others were Belle Vue, Hyde Road (on the Fallowfield line) and Longsight (on the Crewe line). Ashburys was so named because of the nearby railway workshops of the manufacturer and was something of a rarity in that there was no such district of the city. Passenger facilities were dwarfed by the freight operations, the three platforms serving the needs of the suburbs for trains to and from the south and east of Manchester. The two views on this page - February 16th, 1957 - illustrate the 'day to day' operation associated with the Hayfield/Macclesfield services, again in the capable hands of the diminutive Gorton-built 4-4-2 tank engines, on this occasion C14s, No **67441** ***(above)***, and **67447** ***(below)***. With the rear carriages of each of the trains crossing Ashburys West Junction, the ensemble will coast into the station following a sprightly run up the 1 in 173 gradient from Ardwick. The tight curve away from the Crewe line at Ardwick and the allied 35 mph speed restriction, together with a standing start from Ardwick station, will have caused these well-worked veterans a moment of respite. Note in both views the well-filled sidings adjacent to Ardwick West freight yard, particularly the continental wagons which conveyed the oranges from Seville in Spain for the Droylsden firm of Robertsons. ***W A Brown***

Ashburys, 16th February 1957. Once again, that familiar rear end view of a C14 tank, this time No **67441,** with a train off the 'branch', as the Reddish line was known. It was usually bunker first for all trains covering the Hayfield and Macclesfield workings, almost at leisure after the fairly arduous climb into the hills. As well as the freight concentration for this side of Manchester, Ashburys played a very important role in serving the cross city bus services, particularly the 'legendary' No 53 route. The term 'integrated transport', was one for the future, such was the frequency of both rail and road services. The large numbers of engineering companies nearby generated much business, particularly Crossley Brothers. Openshaw Technical School, quite literally the other side of the wall to the right, provided education for numbers of pupils from Bredbury, Romiley, Marple and stations on the Macclesfield line. ***W A Brown***

(Left) For ten years the original Derby Lightweight diesel multiple units were the mainstay of the Hayfield service. Originally with the 'speed-whiskers' on the front, these had been replaced by the small yellow warning panel by March 1965 when this 2-car set was seen at Ashburys on a Hayfield – Manchester Piccadilly working. In the distance, Ashburys East signalbox lies slightly in advance of the junction where the Reddish branch leaves the main line for the 'direct' line to Romiley. This train would have come along this route, indicated by the destination panel, *Manchester via Reddish.* Straight on is the electrified route to Sheffield, shared by Hayfield and Macclesfield line trains travelling via Hyde, as far as Hyde Junction. ***Graham Whitehead***

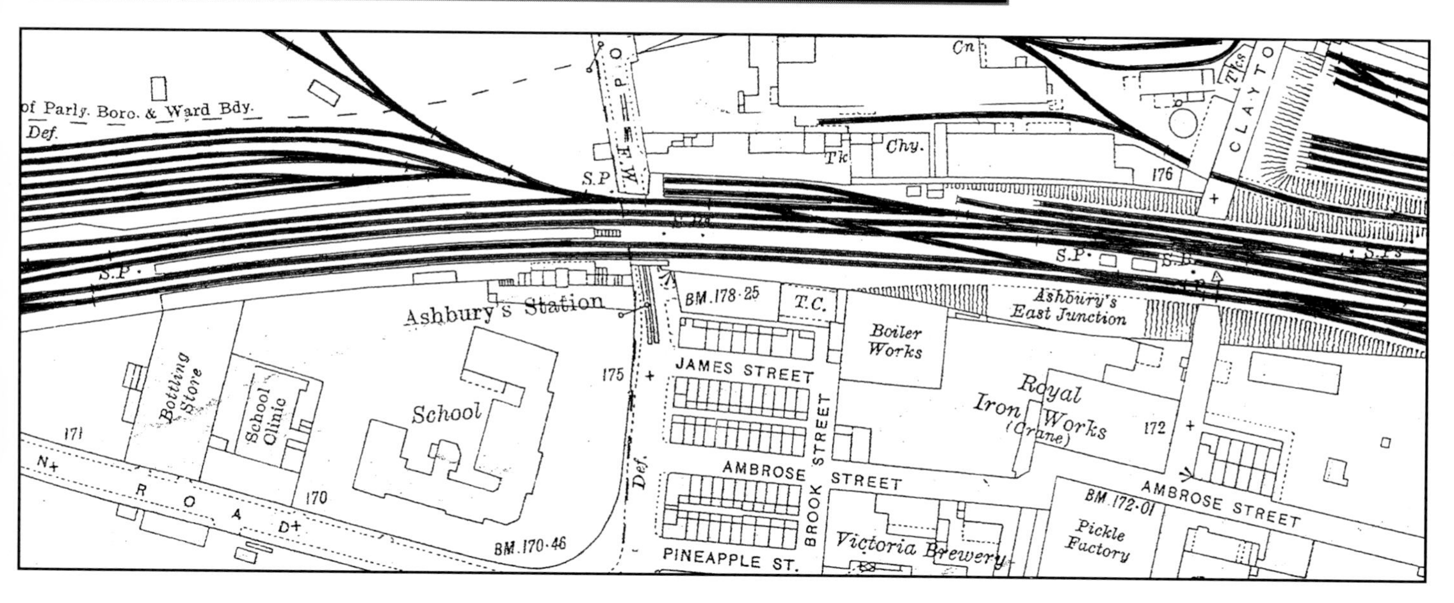

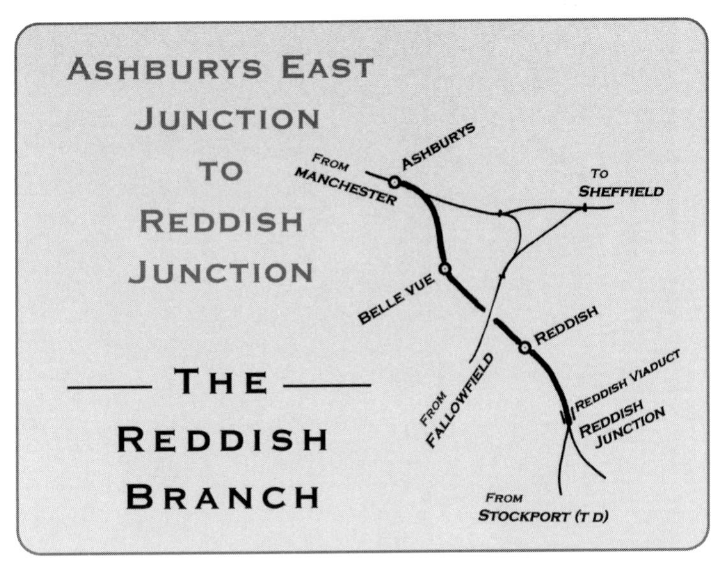

Although acknowledged as part of a direct line from Romiley, the Manchester & Stockport Railway - to give its official title - encompassed two short sections, that from Ashburys East Junction to Reddish Junction, and from there to Romiley Junction. The Reddish Branch, some 4 1/2 miles in length, together with the 2 3/4 miles from Reddish Junction to Romiley, opened from 2nd August 1875. To the traveller, there is no obvious disparity. The line, although jointly owned, had a strong Midland influence, particularly when it came to signalling practices. However, stations and structures as far as Reddish Junction were more in line with MS&L origins. Bridges on the branch were numbered from the Ashburys end whilst mileage distances were calibrated from Ambergate. South of Reddish Junction however, bridges were numbered from Romiley Junction, with mileage calibration from St Pancras. The single station on the section, Bredbury, emanated from the architects section of the Midland Railway Engineers' drawing office, Derby.

Having joined the Reddish branch at Ashburys East Junction, today's travellers will immediately notice a 'low' bush-filled embankment to the left that continues for a few hundred yards. Although the result of a land fill exercise of recent times, it is actually the site of the former Belle Vue engine shed that closed in 1956. Belle Vue was the Midland Railways' Manchester shed (code No. 21) which became 19E under the LMS in 1935. After several changes under British Railways ownership, the shed closed its doors for the last time as 26F on 16th April 1956. The shed itself, dating from 1870, was an early "square" roundhouse which also gave rear access to the eight road fitting shop. Much of the depot building remains, albeit serving different purposes - and is best seen from the adjacent electrified line from Gorton and Guide Bridge.

(Right-centre) This view shows Midland Railway - built Johnson Class 2F 0-6-0 (LMS No **3221**), a design introduced in 1875, in early LMS livery. Note the tender weatherboard to compensate for the short cab roof of the loco. The freshly painted smokebox and chimney suggest that recent minor repairs have been initiated. Above the engine to the left of the picture are the gabled walls of the shed, the entrance being directly above the loco's tender. The two-road coaling stage is to the right whilst the chimney stack to the left of the coal wagon marks the location of the sand drying house. Displaying its 21 shed plate, 3221 was a long time resident of Belle Vue. NEVER REBUILT WITH BELPAIRE BOILER ***P F Cooke***

(Right-lower) On the south side of the coaling stage at Belle Vue shed, this 30th July 1933 view shows another former Midland Railway locomotive, this time a Class 3P 4-4-0 No **743**, in rebuilt form with superheater. To the rear, adjacent to the water column, is Class 2P 0-6-0 No **12121** (Aspinall L&YR No 1081). In the distance, between the locos, is the works of Crossley Brothers, adjacent to Ashburys station. ***Locofotos***

Belle Vue, 7th June 1958. The very considerable expanse of the platforms is highlighted here in this view from the Down platform in the direction of Reddish. From the beginning, the station possessed these impressive facilities to cater for the famous Zoological Gardens just a short distance away. Day to day business was dealt with through the station buildings located at the bottom of what became Glencastle Road. Additional entrances for excursion traffic were located nearer Hyde Road, via a footpath serving platforms 3 and 4 and a side (foot) bridge over the line alongside platform 1. Originally, two signal boxes, North and South, controlled movements through Belle Vue. These were closed on 14th January 1917 when a new box was commissioned at the south end of platform 2. In this picture, despite the presence of new copings and piles of bricks to refurbish platforms walls, the excursion bays were taken out of use in 1963. The decline in popularity and eventual closure in 1977 of the Belle Vue Zoo and Amusement Park resulted in the removal of all but the most basic facilities at the station. Following proposals to construct a new station at Ryder Brow, a decision was also taken to further rationalise the station and relocate nearer to Hyde Road. Work commenced in 1985 with the new facility being brought into use on 12th May 1986. The redundant areas of platform were cut back and the spoil used to fill in the former bay platforms. The footbridge was dismantled and transported to the Midland Railway Centre at Butterley. The present day station occupies the foreground in this picture. ***Stations U K***

The nearby Amusement Park and Zoo were still very popular in the post-war years. Weekends and Bank Holidays generated much revenue for the railway, although on a day to day basis, things were pretty quiet outside the rush hour. Scenes such as we have here were very much the norm. The downward gradient from Ashburys, the presence of Hyde Road bridge and the long sweeping curve to the station had a tendency to muffle the sound of an arriving train. It also on occasion caught the train crew unaware, the squeal of brakes indicating a last minute attempt to stop a platform over-run. Here, a begrimed A5 4-6-2T No **69828** runs alongside the Up platform (No 3) on its way to Hayfield. ***W A Brown***

Belle Vue station was built to accommodate the many excursion trains which brought people to the pleasure gardens and zoo. During holiday times 12 coach trains from Yorkshire, Lancashire and the Potteries would disgorge their passengers and take the empty stock to goods yards for storage until the evening. It was typical for trains arriving at Belle Vue from the north to then proceed to New Mills South Goods Yard or Gowhole (between New Mills and Chinley). The locomotives from all the excursions would then be coupled together and they would be sent via the Midland main line to Heaton Mersey to be serviced. Belle Vue possessed a signal box of Great Central origin, having replaced the two original Midland boxes, Belle Vue North and South (see plans on pages 24/25) in 1917. The view here from the Down platform towards Manchester shows the 36-lever signal box. (on 18th November 1973, along with installations at Reddish Junction and Bredbury, the result of signalling modernisation between Ashburys East and Romiley.) It remained in splendid isolation following rationalisation of facilities at this and many other Manchester Division stations until the beginning of the 1970s· when it closed. ***H C Casserley***

Belle Vue, c.1957. Carrying the headlamp code indicating that this is an "ordinary passenger train", Class A5 4-6-2T No **69806** pauses alongside platform 3 performing such a duty that these engines did so well for the comparatively short time they were based at Gorton. The impressive canopies at Belle Vue provided far superior protection from the elements than almost any other station on the line. However, one abiding memory as a schoolboy (*GF*) waiting for a train is of the damp sulphurous stench that was somehow retained beneath the glazed ironwork. To compound that, the ever present smell of gas from leaking mantles did not encourage one to linger. Few photographs appear to exist showing the goods or coal yard at Belle Vue that was located at the Reddish end of the station. The small yard, on the Down side, had a capacity for 36 wagons. Opening in May 1897, later than most yards on the line, the facility was withdrawn on 15th June 1964. A lie-bye siding on the Down side could hold 25 wagons, whilst the Up side equivalent could hold 43 wagons. ***W A Brown***

The southbound or Up platform at Belle Vue gave all the appearance of being an island platform connected by a lattice footbridge to the northbound platform on which the main facilities were located. There had in fact been a passenger entrance from Hyde Road since the station first opened. The present day entrance uses the same route since relocation of the station in 1986. This view shows the Up platforms from a passing London St Pancras to Manchester Piccadilly train on 20th January 1968, hauled by a 'Peak' (Class 45) diesel locomotive. St Pancras trains were diverted to Piccadilly following the closure of Manchester Central on 31st December 1967, but were short-lived. The closure of the direct line via Millers Dale in July 1968 saw the end of daytime Manchester – St Pancras trains. ***R Gulliver***

An extremely atmospheric departure from Belle Vue is recorded for posterity as 'Jubilee' Class 4-6-0 No **45565** *Victoria* (56F Low Moor) moves away from the platform having disgorged its passengers who have travelled on this excursion from Bradford Exchange (30th August 1965) to enjoy the facilities on offer at the Zoo and Gardens. This Bank Holiday view was typical, weather not withstanding, of the trains that made their way from all parts of the country. The station had seen recent rationalisation following the withdrawal of its goods facilities and the 'layout' was now merely plain Up and Down lines. Both excursion bay platforms had been taken out of use although the footbridge further along the Up platform had been retained pending removal. The operational section of the station would remain at this point for the next twenty years before a decision to re-site refurbished platforms nearer Hyde Road was brought into being. Partially shrouded in smoke, the attractive terra-cotta fronted building of Messrs Kendell & Gent is to the right of the picture. The company enjoyed a reputation for quality engineering and was rail connected from 1920 onwards. Although the factory is long since gone and the site now covered by a housing development, the loading gauge that protected the siding is still standing, albeit hidden by vegetation. ***E F Bentley***

The imposing entrance to Belle Vue station was on the Down side or northbound platform several hundred yards from the Hyde Road entrance along Glencastle Road. This 'Private Road' had a barrier, precluding all but he hardiest of souls who were forced to walk from the station. The station staff at this time (10th June 1965) presumably had a key to enable access for the Vauxhall Cresta RHE 935. Most local passengers however accessed the station from Windsor Street off Mount Road. The station footbridge also provided a short cut across to Williams Street. ***BR(LMR)***

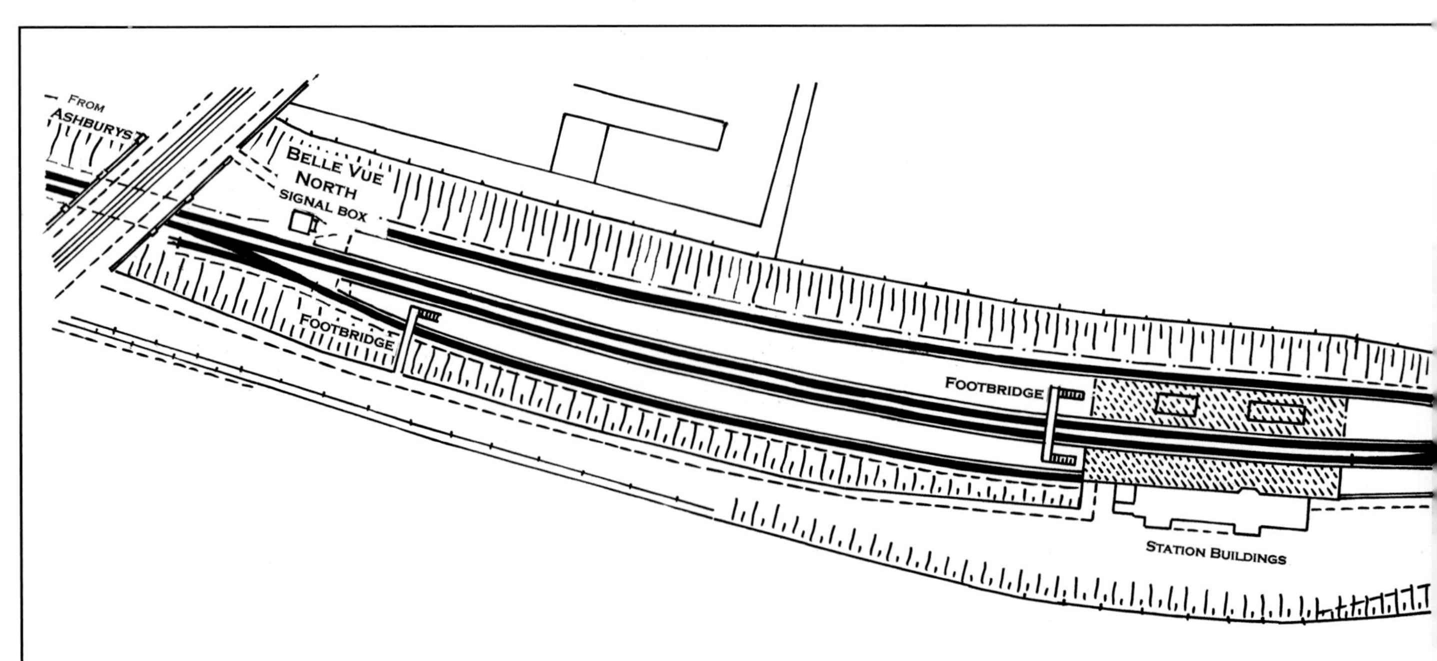

Belle Vue, 10th June 1965. An opportunity to see the main station building detail on the platform side. Cycle and scooter set the period tone and the latest on at the 'flicks'(cinema) included Rock Hudson and Gina Lollobrigida starring in 'Strange Bedfellows' at the Odeon. At the Theatre Royal, in "Cinerama", The 'Flaming Years' was showing. Evidence of a busy station with plenty of advertising, ample seating, and even a Station Master still in residence, (Mr H Burgess). Note the neatly curtained windows overlooking the platform - keeping an eye on the shop ! Return train fare to Manchester before 9.30am was 1/3d (7p); only an eight minute journey to the city ! Off peak fare for the same journey was 1/- (5p) return, with the last train **to** Manchester at 11.45 pm. Posters extol the virtues of train travel to Windermere, North Wales and Ireland. Yes, there were plenty of opportunities to travel by train.

BR(LMR)

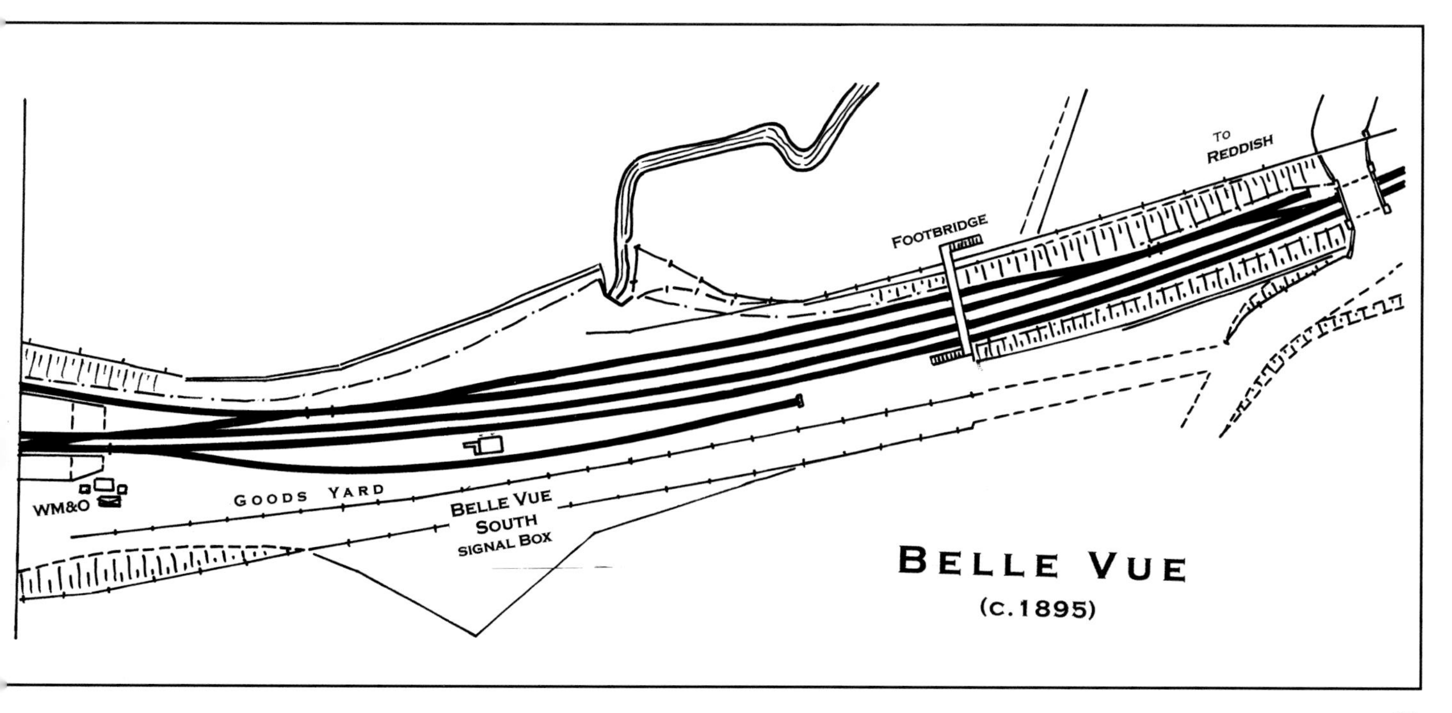

On 10th June 1965, the dimly lit interior of the Booking Office still has that Victorian feeling to it. Many of the Edmondson tickets in the racks had been there for decades, in fact the purchase of a single for the journey from Belle Vue to Ashburys would still have landed a GC&MR marked ticket, no less than forty two years since that undertaking had ceased to exist. It was a fact that more people arrived at Belle Vue than those who commenced their journey there. There was an excellent service into Manchester, but the close proximity of Hyde Road and the procession of town bound buses made for major competition. ***BR(LMR)***

BELLE VUE

(Below) On the Up or southbound platform, passengers facilities were contained in timber buildings custom built within the framework of the cast iron columns. Everything was in need of a re-paint. The light from gas lamps would hardly improve the situation. ***BR(LMR)***

Reddish North

Reddish, second station on the Reddish Branch, was re-named Reddish North on 24th July 1951 to distinguish it from the district's other station on the Heaton Norris to Guide Bridge line. The goods depot had been similarly identified a year earlier on 1st July 1950.

(Right) Reddish station looking north on 20th August 1949. The wrought iron lattice footbridge connects the main buildings on the northbound platform with the less well endowed southbound platform. The large oil lamp proclaims simply 'Reddish' whilst the advert recommends 'Phensic'. An intriguing part of the photograph is the hatted child peeping out from under the cast iron awnings. ***W J Skillern***

Reddish North, 13th June 1959. A view that encompasses virtually all that was on offer at the station. Seen before in an earlier Foxline publication *Railways around Stockport,* it perhaps symbolises a suburban scene of the 1950s. The sturdy features of the Thompson designed Class L1 2-6-4 tank locomotive are shown to fine effect as the 12.10 Manchester London Road to Macclesfield train pulls away from Reddish North, next stop Bredbury. This 1950-built engine was one of a small number drafted into the area to replace the ageing former Great Central types. The small goods yard, with a capacity for 25 wagons, had been closed for traffic some four years earlier (5th September 1955), but was still surprisingly intact. The Great Central built signal box situated at the Romiley end of the Up platform contained a frame of 20 levers; it was closed on the 5th July 1964 but the retaining wall that protected it still remains, albeit hidden beneath the all consuming undergrowth. ***R Keeley***

(Below) On 9th June 1965 LMS built Class 5 4-6-0 No **45307** heads an Ashton Road to Gowhole goods train through Reddish North. This working was but a remnant of the numerous freight trains that once made their way from Manchester over the former Midland lines. The *Working Time Table of Freight Trains between Rowsley and Manchester (and Branches) 15th June to 6th September 1964* highlights the decline in freight traffic over this route with fewer than a dozen workings covering this short stretch between Romiley and Ashburys. The train here left Ashton Road at 10.7am, one of its principal functions being to shunt the yard at Bredbury - Exors of James Mills steel traffic - for which it was allowed fifty one minutes before proceeding south to Gowhole (arr. 11.54).

(Above) A view from cess level of the long straight stretch of line from the Belle Vue direction. The photographer had awaited the passage of the train seen opposite before moving to a position of safety at track level to record the station scene. The signal box dated from June 1911, having replaced an earlier Midland type. Withdrawal of goods facilities from 5th September 1955 reduced its role although it would be another nine years before de-commissioning took place (5th June 1964). Fresh piles of ballast in the 'six-foot' indicate on-going track maintenance at a station that had changed very little over the years. Both: ***Locofotos***

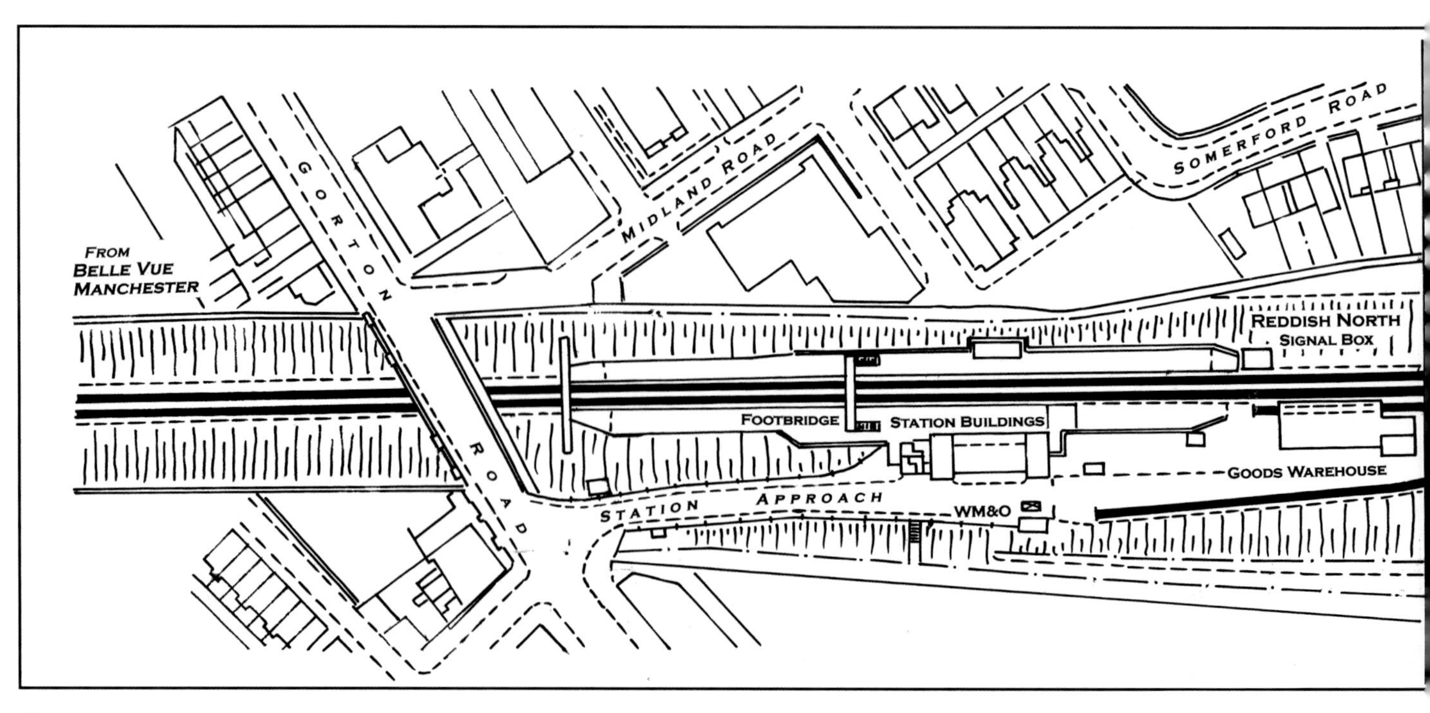

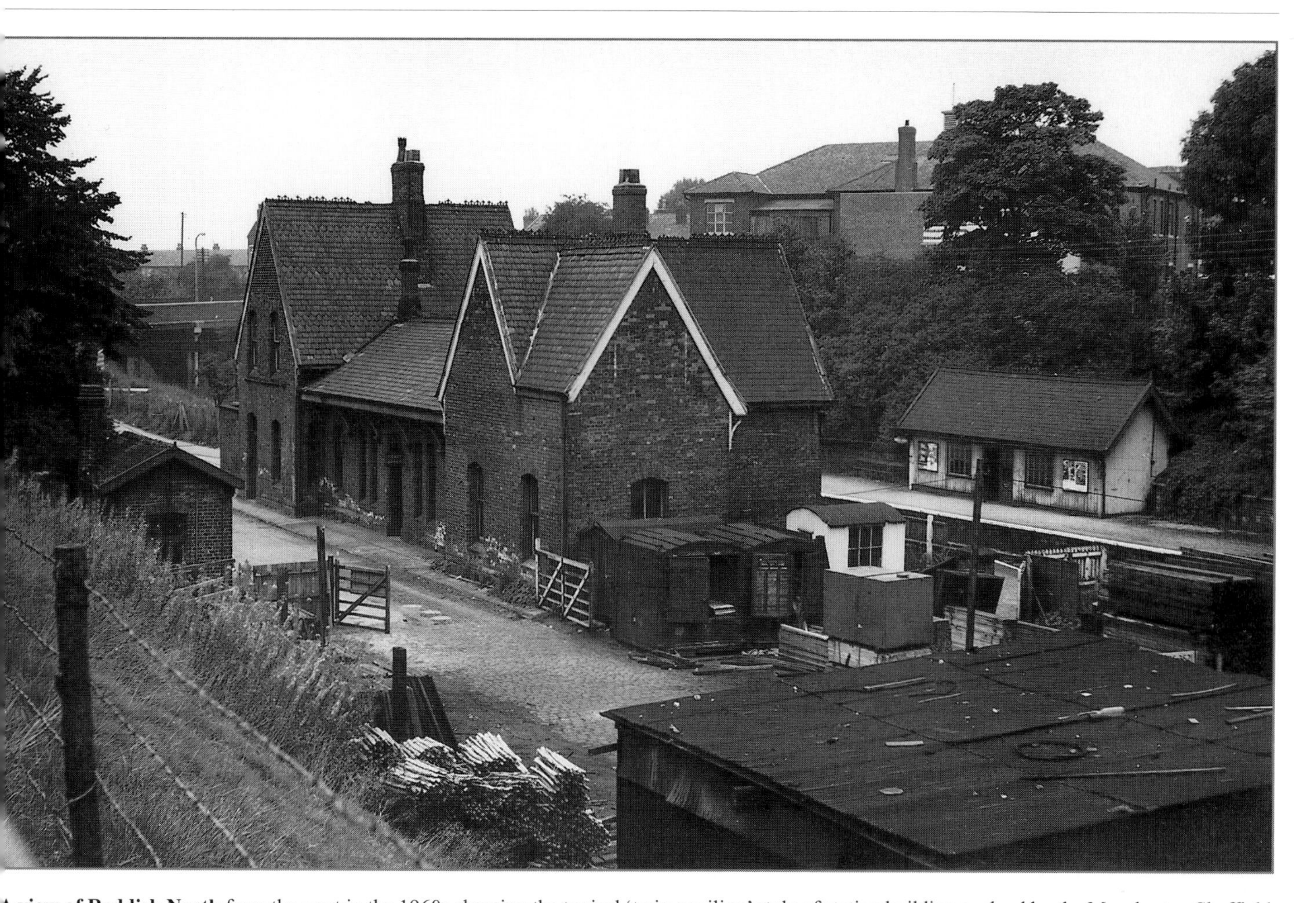

A view of Reddish North from the west in the 1960s showing the typical 'twin-pavilion' style of station building evolved by the Manchester, Sheffield & Lincolnshire Railway. Comprising two projecting gabled end buildings, these 'ends' were connected by section which had a sloping verandah supported by cast iron columns. This feature remains to this day, the remainder of the buildings having been removed. The main buildings were on the Down (northbound) platform to serve the heavy Manchester bound commuter traffic, whilst the wooden waiting room was sufficient for southbound passengers. By this time, the goods yard in the foreground had been let for light industrial use and two early containers were in use for storage. A portable shed with corrugated roof, probably a Lamp Room of Great Central vintage, abuts the station building. A sign in the middle of the station building still proclaims that it is the Ticket Office but generally there is an atmosphere of neglect and decay. These days, Reddish North enjoys a frequent service of trains in both directions to and from Manchester Piccadilly, Sheffield and New Mills. It was different before the advent of diesel services in 1956. The summer of 1949, Manchester commuters enjoyed a good morning peak service with six trains between 7.25 and 9.5; From then on, only five trains were scheduled to call before five'o'clock in the afternoon. With Saturday mornings still being part of the working week, an additional four trains for weekend shoppers, football supporters, etc., ran in the afternoon. Sunday workings appear unbalanced. Southbound there were just three trains, two to Hayfield and one to Marple. Towards Manchester, there were six, four from Hayfield, and one each from Marple and Macclesfield.

Locofotos

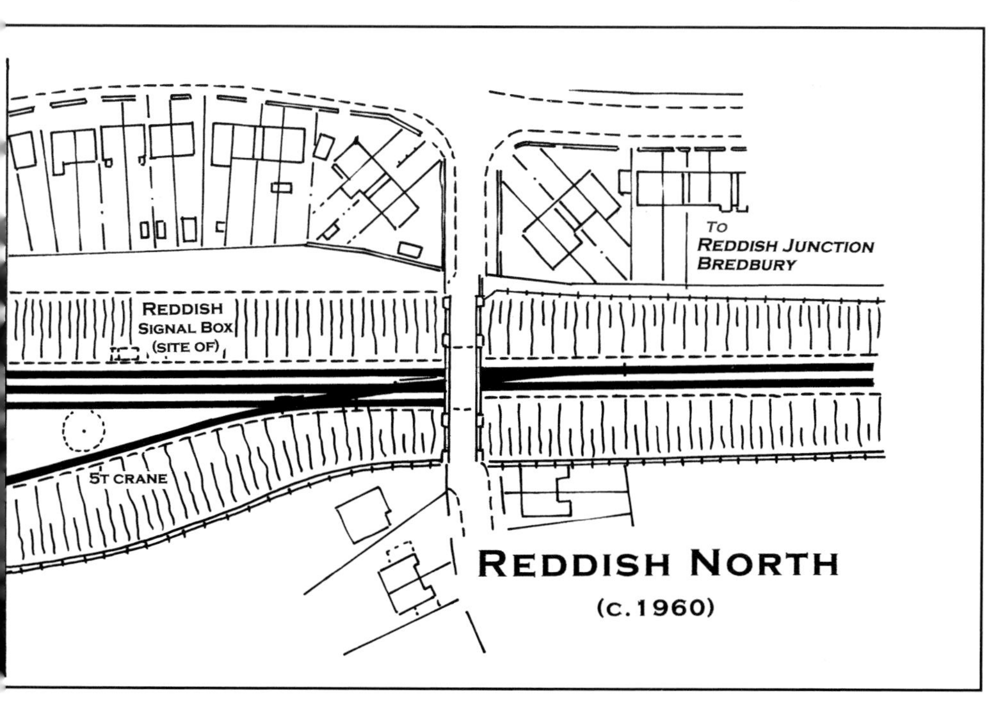

Reddish Viaduct, 31st August 1938. A view that is almost unrecognisable today owing to the growth of vegetation: Reddish Viaduct looking from the south across the Tame Valley. Across the skyline, Reddish had yet to reach the artificial 'town' boundary that had been created by the Heaton Norris to Guide Bridge line. To the extreme right of the picture, the Reddish Branch passed under the quadrupled former LNWR route adjacent to Denton Colliery signal box and a junction serving the pit some distance away in the Haughton Green area. Passengers on the Reddish to Romiley line would have noticed on the left as they emerged from the long intersection bridge the tall embankment of coal ash that had once carried the colliery line. This infill had replaced a timber viaduct at some stage and could frequently be seen 'steaming' due to natural combustion. It was finally landscaped in the 1980s following fires that lasted for several months. The 'sixteen arches' as it is/was locally known is now best viewed from the parallel M60 Motorway. Keen eyed readers will notice a short goods train on the Denton line. In later years the Goods lines were used to stable wagons awaiting repair at the workshops of Standard Wagon at Reddish South.
H L Abel

An early picture postcard produced by J Gould of Reddish shows Reddish Viaduct from the north west, the opposite face to that shown above. Brick-built, it carries the line high above the waters of the River Tame with Manchester/Lancashire on one side and Cheshire on the other. At the southern end (indicated by the signals) was Reddish Junction, marking the beginning of the Brinnington (or Portwood) Branch to Brinnington Junction and subsequently the Cheshire Lines route to Stockport Tiviot Dale. Following the closure of Heaton Mersey Marshalling Yard from the 23rd August 1965, there was only one train using the branch, the 03.25 Parcels train from Stockport Tiviot Dale to Manchester Victoria. With the re-routing of this train via Woodley Junction and Hyde Junction, it would be possible to close the section of line between the CLC at Brinnington Junction and Reddish Junction. Official closure took place on the 7th September 1965, the line subsequently being taken out of use, with points clipped and padlocked, on and from Monday, January 31st 1966. As a result, Gang No 169, which maintained the branch and a section of the line from Reddish Junction towards Bredbury was disbanded, one Ganger being made redundant.
Authors collection

(Above) Reddish Junction looking in the direction of Manchester, circa 1960. LMS-built 4F 0-6-0 No **44119** heads a train of brake vans, probably a balancing working from Ancoats to Gowhole. This part of the line was one which was used to gain speed prior to the ascent to Romiley. Likewise, Manchester bound trains attained their maximum speed as they clattered across the junction and on to the viaduct. The lower quadrant signal, of Midland Railway pattern, the same as the signal box (a 1923 replacement by the LMS), protected the junction to Stockport seen diverging to the left and to the rear of the box. Following the end of Stockport to Manchester train services via this route it was left for the best part of 80 years with little traffic other than nocturnal light engine workings and the occasional stock movement. Its last train ran during 1965. ***Anon***

(Above-centre) Reddish Junction, 26th July 1953. Photographs of the Brinnington branch are few and far between, so a passenger working, albeit in the form of an RCTS railtour was therefore something to be savoured. On this occasion we see L&Y built 2-4-2T No **50644** ready to move away from Reddish Junction - towards Brinnington Junction and Stockport Tiviot Dale - on the next stage of the tour. This 'Manchester and District Rail Tour' had left Manchester London Road at 11.17 that morning and was due to return there at 4.55 in the afternoon, although problems en-route created a 48 minute overall deficit. ***C H A Townley, courtesy J Peden***

(Left) Reddish Junction, n.d; By the nature of the telegraph pole to the rear of the box, the junction had seen much busier days. This view towards Manchester shows the somewhat isolated nature of the box to good effect. This Midland Railway structure, containing a seventeen lever tappet frame, closed on 18th November 1973. ***Scrimgoer Collection/SRS***

Lingard Lane Colliery Sidings signal box was an intermediate block post controlling access to and from the adjacent colliery of that name. One of a number of collieries serving the Bredbury area, Lingard Lane Colliery, better known as 'Bredbury Pit', was the last of the coal mines in the district, closing in 1927. There were two sidings situated on the Up or southbound side with a capacity for 40 wagons and they remained in use, albeit slightly modified, to serve a scrap metal business on the pit site. Today, only a red brick detached house in Lingard Lane survives to remind of the existence of the colliery. The box itself, dating from 1924, closed in October 1966, although a ground frame was retained to serve the scrap metal siding. This view shows the box adjacent to the rear of the Stockport overspill housing development at Brinnington which commenced in the 1950s. In 1976, after years of local pressure, Brinnington got its station. Lingard Lane box is seen here from a southbound train on 20th July 1962; was it Mr. Needham, Relief Signalman on duty that day? ***Graham Whitehead***

(Above) An essay in Great Central nostalgia. An evening commuter train travelling from Manchester London Road to Hayfield is about to cross Ashton Road bridge, Bredbury in 1953. This 'rural' patch of land between Brinnington and Bredbury abounded with the scars of abandoned clay workings, the result of erstwhile brick-making in the area. Nowadays, the location is surrounded by industrial development and much of the foreground has been used for a roundabout which connects with slip roads to and from the M60 motorway. The C13 4-4-2T, with its four wooden bodied Great Central coaches will have been working hard to reach the end of a 1 in 70 gradient from Reddish Junction. The three-quarters of a mile would be at a more acceptable 1 in 130, finishing just before Bredbury. The site in the foreground was also a fan-like spread of earthworks made up of spoil from the approaches to Bredbury Tunnel. ***Eric Oldham***

(Right) A Manchester bound train speeds downhill towards Lingard Lane shortly before crossing Ashton Road bridge, Bredbury. As was usual at the time (c. 1958), only the area around the engine number of the A5 Class 4-6-2 No **69817** has been cleaned. Visible in the distance to the right is the outline of Bredbury Steelworks. Woodley lies to the left of the picture beyond the row of trees which marked the boundary of the abandoned tramway that connected Bents Colliery with Mill Lane. Industrial development has since enveloped the line across this part of Bredbury. ***Rail Archive Stephenson***

(Right) Heading towards Manchester from Bredbury on 12th July 1905 is the LNWR Royal Train conveying the King and Queen from Sheffield to Huyton (near Liverpool) via Manchester Victoria. The train is hauled by two Midland (Deeley) 4-4-0s and is crossing the Cheshire Lines Committee route from Stockport Tiviot Dale to Woodley. The northern-most span in the viaduct bridged a colliery tramway linking Bents Pit (site of the present day Alvanley Clinic) with another site in Mill Lane, Woodley. The 'trammy' as it was affectionately known, crossed the CLC line on the lattice bridge to the right of the picture. Its route could be traced across the fields into the 1950s before Jacksons Brick Works obliterated the alignment. ***R Wood collection***

(Right-centre) Passing the clay pits at Bredbury (to the right out of the picture) Class C14 4-4-2T No **67447** crosses Bredbury viaduct - see the picture above - on its approach to Bredbury station on 21st July 1957. By this time diesel multiple units had taken over a number of workings and most of the GCR built-locomotives had either been withdrawn or sent to the Sheffield area to eke out their last few months. The use of a C14 was therefore noteworthy by this late date. The rolling stock was also changing, for the first two vehicles were BR Mark 1 suburban stock, although the next two were of GCR origin. To the left of the picture we can see the brick kiln chimneys at Brinnington, whilst the wasteland in front belonged to the MOD for many years and provided a testing ground for military equipment such as tanks and other tracked vehicles. ***Norman Harrop***

(Right-lower) Bredbury, 1st March 1947. Stockport Corporation Car No 4, long familiar with Stockport to Hyde regulars, passes beneath Bredbury station bridge on its way towards Woodley. The single track section ran from the bottom of Bents Lane to a point adjacent to the Rising Sun. The low headroom required special wiring attachments and would remain a problem for many years. The bridge was reconstructed and raised in 1976. It was from March 1947 that the trams stopped working through to Hyde, the service being cut back to Bredbury St Marks Church. On May 3rd, that arrangement also ceased, Vernon Park taking over as the limit of services. ***R B Parr***

(Left) Bredbury, 23rd March 1952. The area to th north of Bredbury station still retained much of i rural flavour into the 1950s. There is a sense of calm i this view from the station footbridge as C13 No **6742** crosses Stockport Road bridge to enter Bredbury wi a Sunday service from Manchester London Road. T the right of the engine cab roof are lines of fencin which mark the shallow cutting of the Stockport Woodley line. ***J D Darb***

(Centre) BR 9F 2-10-0 No **92016** struggles to keep heavy southbound goods train moving as it reaches temporary respite in the gradient at Bredbury station c 30th March 1964. The headlamps denote that this is a express freight. At that time, this engine was allocated Newton Heath and it is likely that again the tra originated in north Manchester (Philips Park/Mosto /Middleton Junction) and will run through Chaddesden, near Derby. Just beyond the flat crossing the north end of the platforms can be seen the cent girder of the bridge spanning the Stockport to Hyde roa The signal posts at this time were both of Midlar origin. However, whilst the train has just passed Midland lower quadrant, the starter on the northbour platform has been 'modernised' by the application of BR upper quadrant signal arm. ***Graham Whitehea***

(Below) Bredbury, c.1966. Towards the end of stea Stanier 8F 2-8-0 No **48046** trundles a southbound goo train through Bredbury. With a 9D shedplate on th smoke box, this was a Newton Heath locomotive, th depot now covering local motive power requirements f freight emanating from the Manchester end of the lin The train could possibly have come from nor Manchester, although by now there were only tw booked trips, joining the Reddish to Romiley route Ashburys. At least one of the wagons is coated in lin dust, indicating perhaps that it will probably be bour for the quarries in the Buxton or Peak Forest areas aft sorting at Gowhole. Note the wooden platforms ar buildings, still illuminated by Midland Railway g lamps. Beyond the steel footbridge and boarded crossin the line visibly dips away to the north. ***John Fairclou***

(Above) The northbound or Down platform of Bredbury Station was built on piled timbers overlooking the cutting which contained the line from Bredbury Junction (CLC) up to Romiley. This view, taken on 20th July 1962, shows the platform, the waiting room and footbridge perched precariously over the lower or 'bottom' line, as it was known locally. From above the parapet of Stockport Road bridge, looking towards Romiley, the drainage methods used to keep a stable formation can be seen in the lower centre of the picture. It was during the mid - 1980s with the demolition of Bredbury Steelworks that the infill for the cutting was provided. Redhouse Lane bridge can be seen in the distance.

(Centre) The platform elevation of the Downside waiting rooms at Bredbury can be seen to good effect. Under the platform the land can be seen falling away to the lower line. On the platform, Midland platform seating and gas lights create a period scene. The publicity boards are enticing people to go to the local cinema to see *Barabbas* or to venture to Scotland and travel on the West Highland Line.

(Right) Bredbury station was built on an embankment using wooden platforms and buildings. The brick-built station house, at road level, had a strong Midland influence. This view, dated 20th July 1962, shows the attractive architecture of the house with its varied roof tiles and patterned barge boards. Behind the house, steps led up to the (Up) southbound platform and offices. The wooden ticket office can be seen above the Triumph Herald car on the left.

All; ***Graham Whitehead***

Bredbury, 8th July 1967. A view from the Reddish end of the Down platform, looking south towards Romiley in 1962. Bredbury was the largest provider of traffic on the Romiley to Ashburys section of the route, chiefly due to the presence of the Exors of James Mills steelworks which extended alongside the boundary on the far side of the Bredbury Junction to Romiley line. There was a continual flow of road vehicles, with steel products, across Redhouse Lane bridge, particularly during the hours of darkness. The low platforms here were forever a problem to passengers and it was only with the planned reconstruction of Stockport Road bridge that they were eventually raised. Despite the raising of the platforms and reconstruction of the station in 1976, the waiting room to the right remained defiant, and at its original level. It was finally replaced during 1989/90 with a brick structure to match the main building opposite. The plate girder footbridge was erected in 1914 but still failed to stem the tide of last minute Manchester bound passengers risking their lives to use the barrow crossing at the base of the ramps.

D F Tee

The main station buildings on the Up or southbound platform at Bredbury, 20th July 1962. Built to a Midland prefabricated wooden design it had withstood over eighty years of daily activity. It was in need of a coat of paint but the continued use of cream colouring in an industrial area was never going to help. Access to the platforms was up a long steep flight of stairs adjacent to the footbridge. However, the structure just managed to reach its one hundredth birthday before investment by the GMPTE resulted in new brick buildings and much easier access via ramps and steps. Nevertheless the platform still sported two elegant Handyside manufactured platform seats adopted as standard by the Midland - amongst other railway companies - and a small flower trough. It is interesting to note that the station site was located on one of the numerous open-cast coal mines in the area.

Graham Whitehead

The last product of the famous Beyer Peacock locomotive works at Gorton was the medium powered diesel hydraulic class (known as 'Hymeks') for the Western Region. Later known as Class 35, these locomotives were exclusively allocated to the Western Region and pictures of them operating elsewhere are therefore rare. This makes this picture of **D7051** passing Bredbury on 4th September 1962 rather special. It was unusually in undercoat, on a proving run of eight coaches from Ashburys to Derby. This view from Redhouse Lane bridge shows a large proportion of the goods yard at Bredbury, the long wall of the building to the right once housing the Co-operative Laundry, believed to have been closed in 1947. However, the local bus company, the North Western, was still providing a service from nearby Bents Lane, for workers from Romiley, Compstall and Marple as late as 1960. ***Graham Whitehead***

Bredbury Signalbox was a standard Midland Railway structure dating from 1904. It was on the Down or west side of the line to the south of the station where it faced the goods yard. In this view, dated 19th September 1962, years of grime have darkened the cream paint on the front of the 'box. In the background is Bredbury Steel Works, a significant industrial plant along the route that never had a direct rail connection although a bridge had been considered adjacent to the signal box. The box contained a 20 lever Tumbler frame and was closed on the 18th November 1973. A fire shortly before had resulted in the structure receiving a flat roof. ***Graham Whitehead***

LMS built 4F 0-6-0 No 44080 (allocated to Rowsley) is seen working hard up the line from Bredbury Junction to Romiley on 4th September 1962. This train, carrying an express freight headcode, will probably be re-sorted at Gowhole before the locomotive continues to Rowsley (near Matlock) or Derby. ***Graham Whitehead***

This mid-1960s view shows Bredbury goods depot being serviced by Stanier 'Black Five' 4-6-0 No **45255.** The locomotive was allocated to Newton Heath and this was an interlude in the working of the 10.7am Ancoats to Gowhole, and where steel billets were off-loaded for transfer to James Mills for processing. Passing on the northbound line is a fitted train of box vans. The through line in the goods shed is occupied by steel built mineral wagons for the purpose mentioned above. The goods shed office on the end of the building proved inadequate in later years and supplemented by a sectional timber building across the yard (see page 40). Retired Goods Clerk Harry Foskett, still residing in the Bredbury area, remarked on the volume of traffic created by the Mills organisation, resulting in the need to accommodate additional facilities such as coal at Woodley which was utilised for Coal Concentration for the area along with a scrap metal trans-shipment dock administered by local dealer George Hopwood. ***John Fairclough***

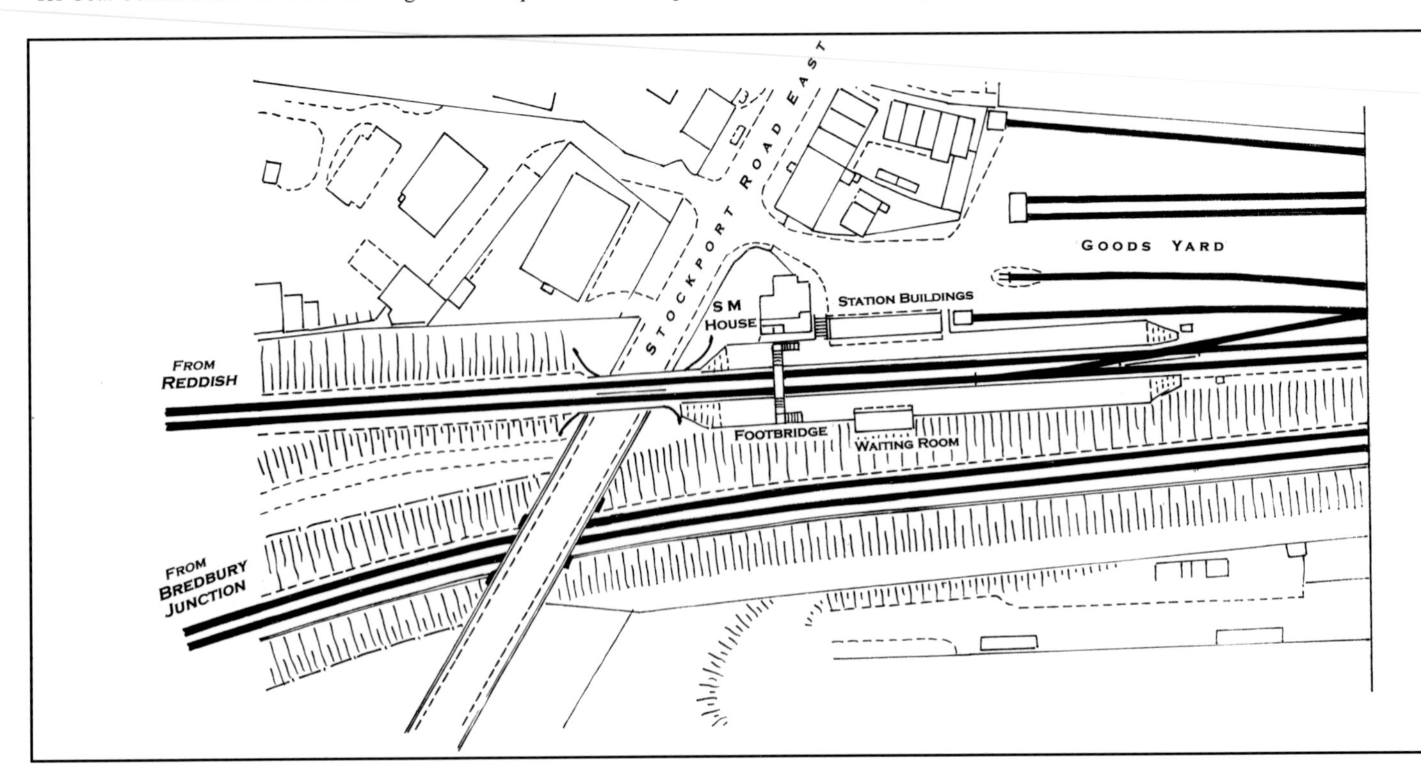

Bredbury, 4th September 1954. A stirring sight is this break with the ordinary as the 'Northern Rubber Special', a train run for the annual staff outing of the Retford based Northern Rubber Company, eases through the platforms at Bredbury on its way to Liverpool (Riverside). Piloted by the preserved Great Northern Ivatt 'Atlantic' No **251**, the train engine is Class D11 'Large Director' 4-4-0 No **62663** *Prince Albert*. According to contemporary reports, this was the first occasion that an Ivatt 'Atlantic' had worked over parts of the route. Having left Retford at 6.15am, the special was due to travel via Worksop, Woodhouse, Sheffield (Midland), Dore & Totley, New Mills, Marple, Manchester Victoria (& Exchange), Newton le Willows and Edge Hill to Liverpool Riverside, due 10.30am. For the the return journey, the train was due away from Liverpool at 8.15pm, with expected time of arrival in Retford being 12.15am on the Sunday. Organiser of the outing was Mr Alan Pegler, later of *Flying Scotsman* fame. ***Anon***

One of the batch of seven Great Central built 4-6-2 tank engines allocated to Gorton at the beginning of 1954 to replace aged C13 and C14 Class 4-4-2Ts, No **69813** stands at the head of a southbound train alongside the Up platform at Bredbury. The one and a quarter miles up a 1 in 93 gradient to Romiley would not present any problems to this powerful engine despite its careworn appearance. To the right of the locomotive is the steel framed corrugated sheet extension to the brick built goods shed that served Bredbury Goods Depot. This and most of the sidings were dismantled in the mid-1970s after local trip workings for James Mills traffic from Ardwick were discontinued. ***W A Brown***

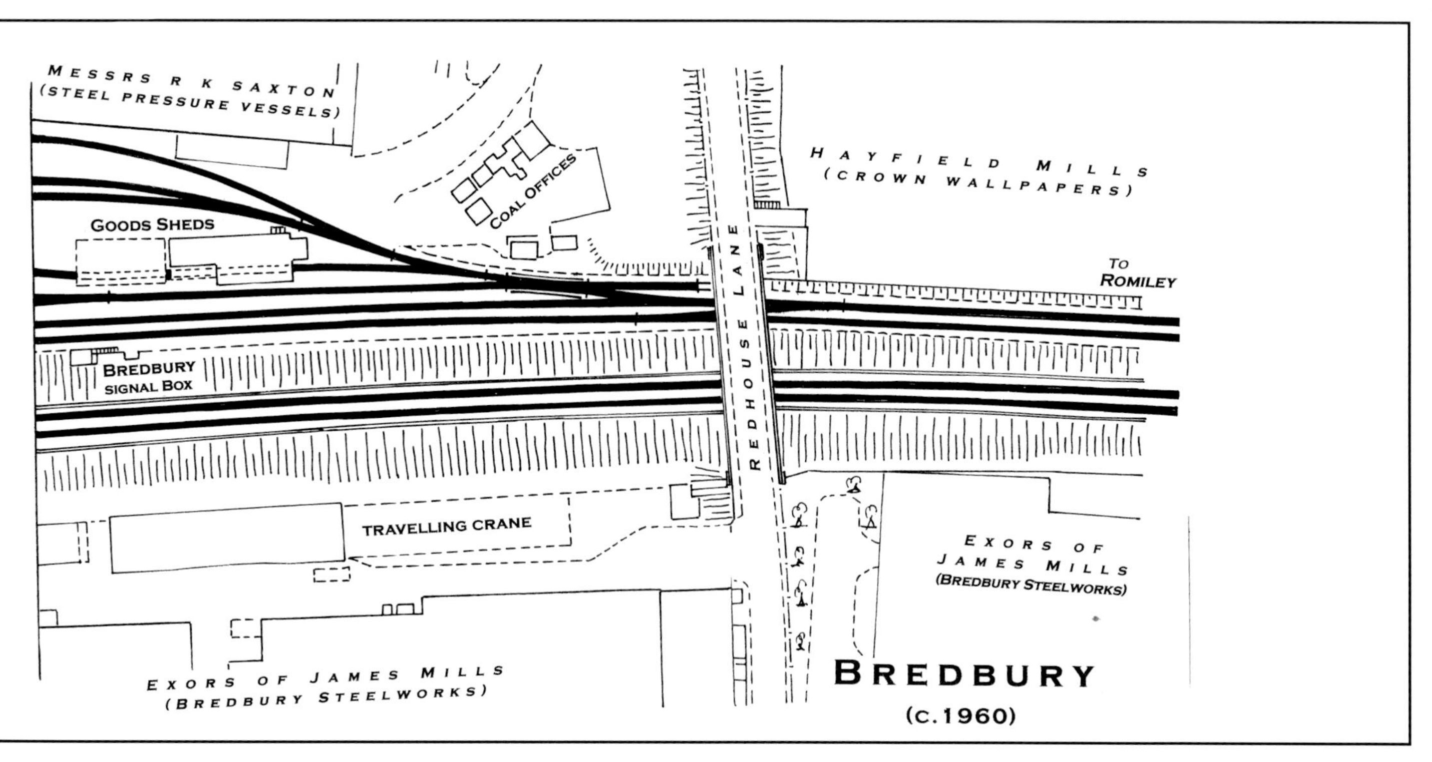

(Right)) British Railways own Electro-magnetic crane is used to transfer steel bars from one of the local lorries contracted by James Mills' for the short distance from the works. Driver Edwin (Ned) Taylor, sits at the controls watching cautiously as other yard operatives perform their tasks. ***Courtesy Mrs Clayton***

(Below) A busy scene at Bredbury goods yard, viewed from Redhouse Lane bridge in the mid-1960s. A BR 9F 2-10-0 is drifting downhill towards Manchester with a goods train containing tubes, probably from Staveley in Derbyshire. An LMS built Class 5MT 4-6-0 is shunting in the goods yard. The painted four character headcode denotes that it has been used recently to haul a Class 1 express, by then a rare occurrence. A Metropolitan Cammell 2-car DMU is pulling away from Bredbury station (seen to the extreme left of the picture) The goods yard, with a capacity for some 80 wagons, had a proliferation of huts used by coal merchants whilst the brick-built goods shed, with its distinctive Midland Railway features (seen above the 9F) was the depot for consignments, although by now principally Mills' smaller commodities. The building adjoining the goods yard was occupied by Messrs R K Saxton Ltd; Pressure Vessel Manufacturers. Behind and parallel to Saxtons was the Rubber and Plastics factory of Messrs Redferns, later British Vita. Bredbury station was quite literally surrounded by industry, but progressively, the companies here and those adjacent, particularly Bredbury Steelworks, have been swept away, in the main to be replaced by housing developments. The sectional timber building to the right of the yard 'shunter' was an extension to the goods yard office given the increasing volume of traffic. The yard ceased to be a public facility from the 29th January 1968 but remained in use as private sidings for Exors of James Mills steel traffic. A local trip working from Ashburys East continued to service this traffic until 1974, possibly 1975. Following closure of the signal box, a crossover was installed on the Reddish side of Stockport Road bridge, controlled by a ground frame - it still exists and present day passengers will note a 'lurch' as their train passes the location - to facilitate this operation. Passengers on the Manchester bound platform could also notice a slight 'curve' along the platform edge where the erstwhile connection to the goods yard was located. ***John Fairclough***

(Above) Bredbury, 20th July 1962. On the bottom line at Bredbury, BR 4MT 2-6-0 No **76085** (a class comparatively rare on this route) is seen drifting down the gradient from Romiley Junction towards Bredbury Junction. Loaded trains traversed this short 1 in 71 gradient cautiously because of a 25mph restriction that was in place for the CLC line to Stockport Tiviot Dale. The bridge carrying Redhouse Lane over over both lines, provided the link between Mills' steelworks - seen running across the right background - and the goods yard at Bredbury. ***Graham Whitehead***

(Right-lower) This mid-1960s view of a ballast train was taken from above the parapets of Redhouse Lane bridge, headed by an ex-LMS 5MT 4-6-0. It is standing at the outer home signal south of Bredbury. The men standing on the wagons are operating the discharge mechanisms which will allow ballast to be fed on to the track. Ahead of the train the line climbs towards the higher of the Bredbury Tunnels. On the right the line from Stockport climbs steeply towards the junction at Romiley. The building on the left was the Bredbury factory of the Crown (formerly Lightbowne Aspinall) Wallpaper organisation. It was also on Redhouse Lane bridge - the station side - that a 'loud-sounding electric bell' (to quote official terminology) was located to warn guards, shunters and others when a train was approaching on the Down line.

John Fairclough

Bredbury, c.1964/65. The less arduous high level line, at 1 in 93, from Bredbury to Romiley, was still a test for trains making a standing start from Bredbury station. By now the long serving former Great Central types had been replaced by more modern counterparts and here we see Gorton (9G) based Fowler tank No **42334** with a Hayfield train approaching Bredbury Tunnel. The housing developments of Queens Road, Newlyn Drive and Victoria Avenue, the latter on the sites of Wards Hat Factory and Bredbury steelworks, border the railway to the left - just out of the picture
John Fairclough

(Below) Bredbury in the early 1950s, Class 5MT 4-6-0 No **44747,** is seen working hard up the 1 in 71 incline from Bredbury Junction, emerging from the lower of the Bredbury tunnels, with a stopping train from Manchester Central to Derby. The locomotive, built at Crewe by British Railways in 1948, was a member of the famed Stanier 'Black Five' Class, as modified by H G Ivatt with Caprotti Valve Gear and Timken Roller bearings. The locomotive was allocated to Bristol Bath Road (22A) at the time but would finish its days in the north-west after a five year stint at Longsight. It is possible that it could have been on a running in turn following overhaul at Derby, although in pre-war (LMS) days, sighting of 'Bristol' Compounds, predecessors to both LMS Jubilees and Class 'Fives' on the Midland route from south-west England was not uncommon in this area because of diagramming which incuded the Manchester run from Derby. It is not clear when this arrangement ceased. On the right is the high level line from Bredbury. The two small boys that can just be seen to the right of the engine were at 'Star Fields', a favourite meeting place for local train 'spotters'. The Royal Mail's Bredbury Sorting Office was located on George Lane in 1970 above the high level tunnel.
B K B Green

Bredbury, 8th May 1948. Still resplendent in its LNER livery, Class C13 4-4-2T No **7403** (BR 67403) bursts from the high level tunnel with a Hayfield bound train. The extremely intrepid photographers undoubtedly had a lineside permit which at the time was fairly common practice for those wishing to pursue their particular interest. No **7403** was one of a batch of 12 locomotives built at the Vulcan Foundry in April 1903 and just managed to fulfil over a half century of service before being withdrawn in August 1954. Both tunnels shared the same number (No 62) despite their being on different lines. ***G Harrop***

(Centre) Approaching Romiley Junction, Class 4F 0-6-0 No **44022,** with Midland tender, 'plods' up the grade with a train of coal 'empties'. It is on the high level line from Bredbury passing over an embankment which took the railway over the Peak Forest Canal (see page 44). The locomotive was allocated for many years to Belle Vue (26G) but was transferred to Newton Heath (26A) in March 1956 when the former depot closed. It has undoubtedly brought the train via Ashburys, probably returning the wagons to the Chesterfield area. ***T Lewis***

Romiley, 19th February, 1949. Another of the numerous trains of empty coal wagons being returned to the East Midlands collieries is hauled tender first by Class J10 0-6-0 No **65157**, a Beyer Peacock & Co built engine of 1897 up the last few yards of the mile and quarter climb from Bredbury Junction. It is possible that these empties have been brought back from Halewood, having originally taken coal for dispersal through the port of Liverpool. Based at Heaton Mersey, the J10 would have been familiar to the local trip workings that emanated from the depot. Those familiar with the locality these days will notice how vegetation has proliferated where once the trains ran. ***J D Darby***

(Above) Running light engine back to Manchester on the Romiley Junction to Reddish line towards Bredbury, an ex-LMS 4F 0-6-0 has probably left its goods train at Gowhole. This view, dated 3rd July 1949, shows the Romiley to Hyde section of the Peak Forest Canal. A bridge, dating from 1874, takes the canal under both the Reddish and Bredbury Junction lines. A view of the railway from the towpath adjacent to Stockport Road canal bridge at Romiley is now impossible given the development and growth of vegetation over the last three decades. ***H Townley***

(Right-centre) This view through bridge No 61 towards Romiley along the towpath of the Peak Forest Canal shows both the original structure and new support arch - with concrete invert - constructed in 1930 to repair damage caused to the arch beneath the lower (Bredbury Junction) line. The cover - beneath the sleepers - at this point had always been shallow but the constant passage of heavy trains eventually resulted in severe cracking and the need to repair the structure. The span of the new arch was just twenty feet, some ten feet smaller than the original. ***Authors collection***

(Right-lower) An afternoon Manchester Central to Derby stopping train forces itself over the last few yards of the incline from Bredbury Junction to Romiley along the low level line in the early - 1950s. The locomotive, ex-LMS 'Jubilee' Class 6P5F 4-6-0 No **45696** *Arethusa*, was allocated to Derby until 1952. It was one of a batch built at Crewe in 1936 and was attached to a 3,500 gallon Fowler-style narrow tender, which it gained when this type was discarded by the 'Royal Scot' Class locomotives. ***J D Darby***

Romiley, c. 1955. Some time in the mid-1950s, this view from Quarry Road bridge on the approach to Romiley Junction - on the line from Bredbury - is ex-LMS Fowler/Hughes 5MT 2-6-0 No **42750** of Newton Heath. This is a train of empty coal wagons which the locomotive would take as far as Gowhole, handing over to another locomotive for the final stage of the journey back to the Chesterfield area. On the right the "Old route" from Manchester via Hyde is seen approaching the junction. At the time, the organisation of the railways was still very much the same as that prior to the 1948 nationalisation. The train is just about to leave the Manchester District and enter former "Midland" territory which started a few yards to the north of Quarry Road bridge. Until 1966, a white marker post, located on the Down side of the 'bottom' line, had indicated that here was the boundary between the Derby North (the former Ambergate District) and Manchester Districts. A major reorganisation of 1966 resulted in the creation of 'Divisions' of British Railways that completely altered the 'geography' of the area. A new and enlarged Manchester Division emerged which extended its boundaries further south, as far as Totley on the Hope Valley line and Millers Dale on the Derby line, where it shared a boundary with the new Sheffied (ER) and Nottingham (LMR) Divisions respectively. *Anon*

(Right-lower) Romiley, 18th August 1955 (Sat). Passenger services to and from the former Midland lines were placed in the hands of a variety of motive power, especially Saturdays during the summer months when excursion requirements demanded maximum availability of motive power. No details of the train seen here are available other than the assumption that its last port of call was Stockport Tiviot Dale. With the possibility that it could be bound for either Derby or Sheffield, the reason why LMS built Class 4F No **44066**, a Staveley (18D) based engine is in charge, remains a subject for debate. It carries the headlamp for an ordinary passenger train. *E R Morten*

ROMILEY

The privatisation of British Rail brought about many changes, some welcome, some otherwise. The various colour schemes of the train operating companies that emerged however brought memories of the 1948 nationalisation period when locomotives were still operating in the colours of the 'big four'. An LNER Class B1 in Apple Green livery must have been a stirring sight as it passed through Romiley, a welcome change from the run of the mill tank engines that were the regular workhorses for the majority of passenger trains. The upper picture, the first of three taken on the 8th May 1948, shows North British built B1 4-6-0 No **1225,** in lined green livery, clearing Quarry Road bridge on the Reddish line with a return Hayfield to Manchester working. The bridge, a short distance from Romiley station, has always been popular with photographers, given the confluence of the three routes. In the centre, C13 4-4-2T No **67437** takes advantage of the falling grade (1 in 1100) - a welcome change from the hard work needed to make the outward journey - to move away from Romiley on the Hyde line. The lower picture shows another Class B1, this time No **1223,** easing off in readiness to cross the junction, with its 20mph speed restriction, at Romiley station. These turns were intended to run up mileages while the engines were being prepared for main line running. ***G Harrop***

(Right) Romiley, 15th March 1952. The high embankment between Woodley and Romiley ran parallel for most of its length with the Peak Forest Canal. Its elevated position also gave good views across the Cheshire Plain. Here we see 'push and pull' fitted C13 No **67438** round the thirty chain curve with a train bound for Hayfield. ***J D Darby***

(Below) Romiley, 1949. A Saturday afternoon train from Manchester London Road to Macclesfield Central comes off the Hyde line on the approach to Romiley Junction in 1949 headed by J11 (GCR Class 9J) 0-6-0 No **64298** of Gorton. The four coaches are all pre-Grouping in origin, the first and third being Great Central whilst the second is a Great Eastern coach. The Romiley outer home signal is a wooden Midland lower quadrant. The fencing in the upper right of the picture also marked the boundary of a small quarry which in wartime served as the local rifle range for a local detachment of the Home Guard. ***Eric Oldham***

(Above & Below) Romiley, 13th August 1955. The elevated vantage point offered by Quarry Road is again used to great advantage to view the railway from the south. By coincidence, different photographers have visited the location on the same day to record what can be generally accepted as an everyday scene of life at Romiley. The view above by ***E R Morten*** shows Class C13 No **67431** approaching Romiley from the Hyde line, possibly with a train for Hayfield. Below we see the composition of ***W A Brown*** who on this occasion chose a position at the other end of the bridge to obtain a fine panoramic view of the three lines as they left Romiley, Hyde to the left, Reddish in the centre, Bredbury Junction and Stockport Tiviot Dale in the right foreground. Almost of passing interest, the train just happens to be a Macclesfield Central to Manchester London Road via Reddish working.

Romiley Junction to Hyde Junction The "Hyde Loop"

(Above-right) Romiley Junction, c.1966; as seen from a train heading for Manchester Central along the lower line to Stockport. The site of the goods yard (closed 30th January 1965) has been cleared and demolition of the cluster of buildings would soon follow. The line straight on is the original or "Old" route to Manchester via Hyde, whilst the middle route is the line to Reddish Junction and Ashburys. ***M S Cross***

(Centre) Romiley, 13th August 1955. Quarry Road bridge once again provides the vantage point for this excellent view of the three routes leaving Romiley Junction. On this occasion, C14 4-4-2T No **67445** effortlessly hauls its Hayfield to Manchester London Road train of five carriages on the next stage of its journey towards Woodley. ***E R Morten***

(Right-lower) By 1951, the Romiley outer home signal on the Hyde line had been replaced by one of a standard BR upper quadrant design. Waiting to head towards Hyde is a former Midland Railway 3F 0-6-0 whilst approaching from Hyde is a Manchester London Road – Hayfield train headed by C14 (GCR Class 9L) 4-4-2T No **67447**. A batch of these locomotives was drafted to Gorton shortly after Nationalisation, coming to the aid of their older C13 counterparts. ***Eric Oldham***

A BRIEF DESCRIPTION OF THE ROUTE

Our return to Manchester involves taking the 'Old' route via Hyde and Guide Bridge. Only a handful of trains actually take this route from Hayfield which, at 18¼ miles, is some 3 miles longer than the more direct route via Reddish. From Romiley, the route ahead for Woodley follows a straight course with both sets of lines from Bredbury Junction and then Reddish Junction respectively bearing off to the left immediately beyond the signal box. Once again, a high embankment position gives elevated views of Romiley village to the left with the gentle slopes beneath Healdwood and Greave descending from the right. A local landmark in the form of the unique flat-topped houses hold a prominent position on 'Top o' th' hill' as we quickly reach the three arched overbridge (No.60; Quarry Road). Whilst the other routes fall away to our left, we take a long sweeping curve in a north-westerly direction between rocky outcrops on a rising gradient of 1 in 1100 which will last at least another mile. With the hillside slopes encroaching steeply on our right, the route ahead transfers on to a lofty embankment as the Peak Forest Canal emerges down on our left from the short tunnel which has passed beneath the other two lines. The wooded slopes on the right will stay with us for something like a quarter of a mile as we run parallel with the canal. The line now takes a straight course and enters a long shallow cutting at Gilbert Bank (No.34) that will end shortly before Woodley station. A series of overbridges criss-cross the line ahead of us as our train seeks power from its engines to maintain momentum on the rising gradient. The first bridge, a skew built stone arch (No.35; High Lane) marks the start of an area of land to our right known as the "LNER", a sports ground with cricket (*later Woodley*) and hockey pitches provided and maintained for British Railways teams by the organisation. As the name suggests, it was provided at a time when sporting activities were a major welfare consideration of the various railway companies. A footpath opposite the Werneth Road end of Station Road provided convenient access from Woodley station. Prior to housing development to the left of the line, a footbridge (No.36) also crossed the line giving access to the sports field. This was removed, it is believed, in the 1930s. The next bridge (No.37; Werneth Road), is where the cutting opens out to accommodate four lines, the two outer being loops for goods trains. A small covered signal frame occupies a site to our left hard up against the bridge wing wall. Until 1936, as Woodley South, it was one of three signal boxes serving **Woodley**. As we approach the junction, we also reach the furthest point calibrated from London St Pancras at 179½ miles. Opposite Woodley Junction box, the line curving in from our left is the Cheshire Lines route, at 40¼ miles from Liverpool Central. The village of Woodley lies between the stations of Bredbury and Woodley and has perhaps always been better served by train services on the Reddish line. The merging of the routes from Stockport and Romiley forms an end on connection with the Hyde Branch at a point some 8¾ miles from Manchester London Road. There is a small goods yard to our left behind the station buildings, two sidings provided by the CLC and goods shed by the Sheffield & Midland Committee. The brick buildings are substantial, inclusive of the Station Masters House, Booking Office, Waiting Rooms and other accommodation for the railway business. The platforms are short and low, unlike any others on the line. The route ahead continues to be straight but the slight adverse gradient requires extra output from the dmu's engines which are amplified as we pass beneath Hyde Road bridge (No.22) and into another shallow cutting. The gradient now changes to our advantage and it will be downhill as far as Apethorne Junction. The open nature of the countryside opening out to our left, a combination of Cheshire landscape and Manchester's urban sprawl, is as yet only disturbed by the odd building, the first of which is a former cotton mill but now the premises of Messrs Norman Evans & Rais. The tall stone edifice that is **Apethorne Junction** signal box appears on our left and marks the point at which the line to Godley Junction forms a fragmented section of the CLC but nevertheless important link with the Woodhead route across the Pennines. Just as imposing is the red brick mass of Gee Cross (Gee X) Mill to our left. We continue downhill at speed, through pleasant woodland, on a gentle long sweeping curve. The rural surroundings come to rather an abrupt end as we enter a short cutting and pass beneath Croft Street bridge (No.11) to enter Hyde. On the left are the uniquely dated walls of Joseph Adamsons - Boilermakers, a long established Hyde company. The large goods yard to the right offers a form of barrier between the railway and the town. **Hyde Central** station is approached as a gradient change occurs, the slight ascent helping our train to ease to a halt with minimal braking. Much of the station is built on a viaduct with the main entrance on the Up side in Great Norbury Street. The elevated position again gives panoramic views across east Cheshire as we leave the station and across Manchester Road, now heading due north. The start of a long gradual curve brings us to the end of the viaduct and towards a shallow cutting as the land rises to our right and the site of another long established Hyde company, that of Fletcher Miller *(later Burmah Castrol - one time Tinker Shenton Iron Works),* oil based products. A private siding to serve these works was installed in 1916. Now climbing steadily, the 1 in 150 climb will control our approach to the platforms at **Hyde North** station. The substantial stone buildings share a similarity with others on the Sheffield line but are in distinct contrast with the wooden shelter on the platform opposite. However, the most notable imposition is the overhead equipment resulting from the Manchester, Sheffield and Wath project of recent years. Hyde Junction marks the end of our short journey over the 'Hyde Loop'.

Hyde North, 18th April 1954. The route for Hyde and Romiley leaves the Manchester to Sheffield line at Hyde Junction. The approach to the station is up a short 1 in 97 gradient, something of an imposition after having to recover from the 15mph restriction across the junction. Class C14 4-4-2T No **67447** enters the station with a southbound train. The premises of Messrs Daniel Adamson fills the right of the picture. The name change to Hyde North (*from Hyde Junction*) took place on 17th September 1951. ***H C Casserley***

Woodley, c.1955. From the elevated position of Buckleys bridge (No.38), an occupation bridge now removed, an excellent overall view of Woodley from the south is obtained in the decade before rationalisation on a large scale began to bite. A Class C13 4-4-2T No **67427** has the easiest of tasks as it pulls away from Woodley with a Manchester London Road to Macclesfield Central train, a 22¼ mile journey taking in fourteen stations en route. Overall journey times varied between 54 minutes (early morning with the first stop at Guide Bridge), and 63 minutes for an all stations service. The weekday service provided for eleven trains between Manchester and Macclesfield via Guide Bridge with eight on Sundays. The Loop lines, although available for goods trains, were generally used as an 'overflow' for the goods yard, hence the presence of the three coal wagons to the left. The number of wagons in the goods yard suggests plenty of activity. Station Road runs along the top of the embankment on the right, providing a connection between Hyde Road and Werneth Road (for the sports ground) although access from the latter was restricted by a gate due to the one-time 'private' status of the road.

W A Brown

Woodley Junction, 14th September 1965. Trains entering or leaving the Stockport line to the right were governed by a 10mph speed restriction and here we see Stanier Class 8F 2-8-0 heading light-engine for Stockport. The junction signals by now had been relocated to a point 177yards on the Hyde side of Woodley, which offered more protection for the station. At one time however, engines approaching Woodley from the Hyde direction were required to sound three whistles if they were bound for the Stockport line and one whistle for the Romiley line. Woodley Junction signal box, built by the Manchester, Sheffield & Lincolnshire Railway, was commissioned on 15th December 1895 and contained a Dutton tappet frame of 50 levers. It will be noticed here that direct access to the Up Loop has been removed and the truncated line reduced to siding status; the Down Loop was similarly affected. Further rationalisation however would be of a temporary nature until closure of nearby Apethorne Junction box in 1966, which resulted in Woodley box taking over control of signalling at that location. However, the decline in freight traffic resulting from closure of the Woodhead route, and a decision to abandon the Cheshire Lines route through Stockport following temporary closure of Tiviot Dale Tunnel (due to motorway construction problems), ultimately brought about the demise of the box, closure taking place on 21st September 1985. The line to Romiley continues straight ahead. The former Woodley South signal box was located immediately beyond the first arch bridge. Note also the positions of the toilets, those serving the public quite naturally at platform level, whilst the signalman had his own facility up the embankment. The poster board to the left advertises 'Football at Edgeley Park' where 'County' (Stockport) were to take on Chesterfield. The 'sixties' highlighted the highs and lows of the club, as most local supporters will know too well.

D A Davies

Woodley, c.1960. A view from the station footbridge (No.23; Hyde Branch) looking south. A train has just departed for Romiley leaving the station staff to discuss a matter on the platform. Just coming into sight from the CLC route from Stockport Tiviot Dale is a Class J39 0-6-0. A number of these were allocated to Gorton, sharing duties, albeit infrequently, with J11s on the Hayfield line goods trains. Woodley Station had a brick-built station master's house and administration block dating from 1862. The wing at the south end was a later addition. The Waiting Shelter and signal box on the Up (southbound) side are of MS&L origin although platform furniture and fittings are more in keeping with Midland taste. In earlier days the goods yard was shared between the Sheffield & Midland Joint undertaking, who had a single siding to the goods shed, and the CLC which had two sidings, mainly for coal. It is on record that in 1868, the station provided employment for no less than sixty eight staff. ***Dr I Scrimgeour***

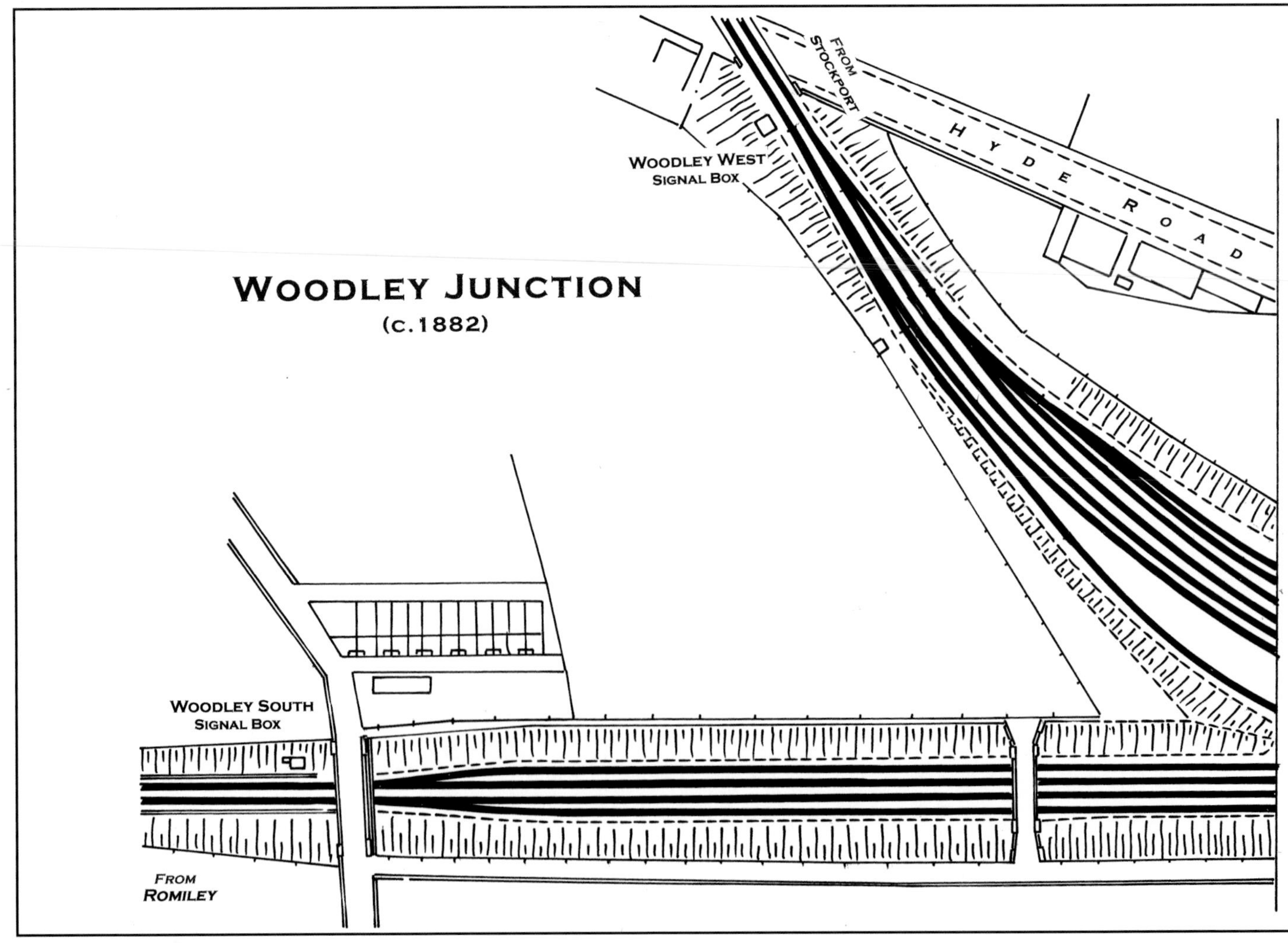

BUILT LMS CREWE 1935. WDRN. 1965.
CREWE N. 1937, DERBY 1944, TRAFFORD PK. 1948
NEWTON HEATH 1960

Woodley

(Right) 'Jubilee' Class 4-6-0 No **45652** *Hawke* (9E; Trafford Park) accelerates south through Woodley Station with a diverted Manchester Central–London St Pancras train in the early 1950s. On the left is the the goods shed, of a similar design to those at Hayfield, Strines and Marple. The locomotive is crossing the junction with the line to Stockport Tiviot Dale, which curves away to the bottom left hand corner of the photograph. The outward route, via the Fallowfield Loop, Guide Bridge and Hyde, provided a convenient alternative to the Midland main line during engineering possessions north of Chinley. However, it really came into its own in the late 1950s when modernisation of the west coast route for electrification between London Euston and the North-West was in full swing. ***Eric Oldham***

(Above) The main entrance to the station was situated on the west side adjacent to Hyde Road. The doorway seen here gave access to a long Booking Hall into which was set a small window from which the tickets were issued. At the time of the picture, 25th August 1974, a regular interval service was in operation throughout the day, a somehat different situation than that of twenty years previously. In 1954, Woodley had enjoyed good Monday to Friday morning and evening services to and from Manchester, but suffered during the off-peak period after 8.43am with a gap of over two hours before the arrival of the 10.52. The next train to Manchester was 2.14pm in the afternoon ! There was a modest improvement on Saturdays with a train at 12.45pm. On Sundays, there were nine trains to Manchester, four originating at Hayfield and five at Macclesfield. Southbound, a total of eleven called at Woodley, five to Hayfield and six to Macclesfield. ***M A King***

(Below) Woodley station master's house and administration block on the Down (northbound) platform are seen in this view from a passing train on the 18th April 1954. Just beyond the road bridge (No.22; Hyde Road) can be seen an early example of a colour light signal. It was constructed to an LNER design in the 1920s and was interesting in that it was operated by a traditional lever mechanism. ***H C Casserley***

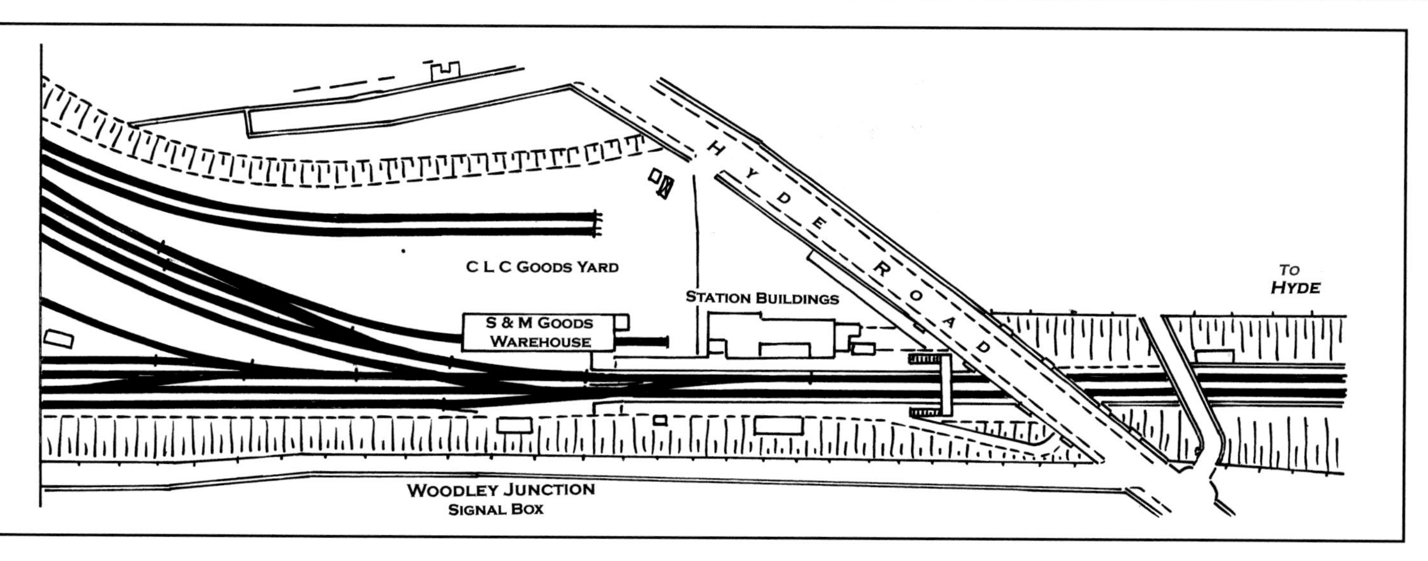

Apethorne Junction was located some 661 yards north of Woodley Junction towards the end of a section of the Hyde Branch with a falling gradient of 1 in 117 northbound. It was the point at which the Cheshire Lines Committee recommenced its west to east route towards Godley Junction on the cross-Pennine route between Manchester and Sheffield. In contrast, the route from Godley Junction descended sharply towards Apethorne Junction at 1 in 100, giving rise to potential difficulties for trains travelling in either direction, particularly loose-coupled freights. The opening by the CLC of the 2 1/4 mile section of line to Godley Junction in 1866 resulted in this awkward arrangement. It is somewhat thought provoking that the permissible line speed between the two points was 60mph. There was a speed restriction of 25mph through the junction for trains to and from the Godley line although in most instances, trains rarely exceeded or even approached that. The differing and opposing gradients of the two lines, and the overbridge, resulted in sighting problems for both signalman and train crews alike, hence the tall structure.

(Above-right) The open countryside around the Apethorne area of Hyde made for an attractive setting into which the railway fitted comfortably. This view in the direction of Hyde shows BR Standard Class 9F 2-10-0 No **92105** (8H - Birkenhead) negotiating its train from the Godley line at Apethorne Junction. The train, consisting of 'Conflats', an assorted mixture of covered vans and bogie bolsters at the rear, is possibly running partially fitted (braked). Apethorne Junction box was in the last few months of its operational life, closing on 12th June 1966 when control was transferred to Woodley Junction. Note also that the route is cleared for a train to take the Godley line from the Woodley direction. ***A K Rathbone***

(Above-left) Trailing off the CLC line from Godley Junction, Class 8F 2-8-0 No **48673** (9B-Stockport) joins the Hyde–Romiley line at Apethorne Junction in the summer of 1967. Almost immediately, the locomotive will face an adverse gradient to Woodley before branching off on to the steep downhill section to Stockport Tiviot Dale. This was a train of coal from Yorkshire to Garston and part of a regular flow travelling this way via the Woodhead route until that line closed in 1981. ***Ian R Smith*** **(Above-right)** Northwich based Stanier 8F 2-8-0 No **48398** proceeds cautiously downhill towards Apethorne Junction with a train containing an assortment of wagons, a number of which are empty 'Covhops' on their way back to ICI plants in the Northwich area. Photographed from Apethorne Lane bridge in the direction of Godley, we see the recent housing development around the outskirts of Hyde, Foxholes Road to the left, Cheetham Fold Road to the right. The line closed to all traffic from 20th July 1981. ***A K Rathbone***

Hyde Central

(Right) A view looking south from Hyde Central on 18th April 1954 with Croft Street bridge visible in the distance. The station was the original terminus of a short-lived branch from Hyde Junction in 1851. Part of a scheme to reach Whaley Bridge, it fell foul of the bursting of the bubble in railway investment, and the line was taken up in 1858. However, it was revived as part of a branch to Marple and re-opened in 1862. In this view the engineering firm of Joseph Adamson (on the right) had regular deliveries of goods by rail until the mid-1960s. Also to the right but out of the picture is the Peak Forest Canal. The goods yard was on the left hand side of the train. Although the public goods facilities were withdrawn on 21st May 1966, use of the sidings continued in private hands for a short time. Hyde Central signal box closed on the 23rd March 1969. ***H C Casserley***

(Left) Class C14 4-4-2T No **67450** pauses alongside the Up (southbound) platform on 17th May 1957 prior to departing with the 3.5pm Manchester London Road to Macclesfield train. It has taken all of twenty four minutes to travel the first seven and a half miles of a twenty two mile journey, a leisurely schedule to say the least. Of the fourteen weekday southbound trains booked to call, eight were destined for the Macclesfield line with a small number terminating at Rose Hill. The remainder took the New Mills line, some terminating at Marple but most continuing through to Hayfield. The engine, built by Beyer Peacock for the Great Central Railway (Class 9L) in June 1907, was the last surviving member of the class, being withdrawn in January 1960. ***W A Brown***

(Centre) Known simply as 'Hyde' originally, the station was renamed Hyde Central on 17th September 1951. The goods yard had already received its new name on 1st July 1950. This view is from the Down (northbound) platform serving trains for Guide Bridge and Manchester. The platforms were connected by a boarded enclosure (giving the effect of a subway) through an arch of the viaduct in the centre of the station. A canopy, seen here to the left, was later built over the 'subway' entrance which reached the platform via an enclosed cantilevered stairway. The main buildings, on the Up side, were built in 1862 for the Marple extension. In this September 1966 view, the buildings are suffering the effects of age, the canopy in need of additional support. Scaffolding around the chimney stack highlights ongoing maintenance problems. Rationalisation in the early 1970s resulted in demolition of these buildings and provision of new facilities on a more limited scale. ***G Biddle***

Hyde Central, August 1960. The Down platform at the start of August 'Wakes', the annual holiday period for the people of Hyde and district when the town and outlying areas would empty as the local population sought to escape to the seaside. A crowded platform with groups of all ages full of expectation. The expressions give a cautious acknowledgement to the camera, with somewhat mild indignation from some of the young men to the right. 'Sunday best' is the order of the day as far as clothing is concerned, with collar, tie and suit (or sports jacket) for the men and long coats for the ladies and young girls. Not a pair of trainers or designer label in sight ! This was a scene repeated annually before the advent of holidays abroad, although little did we know of the changes that would soon be taking place. Allied with arrangements made for the Stockport and district 'Wakes', British Railways provided a number of special trains although the handbill identifies only four which were specifically designed to serve Hyde. On the Friday evening (12th August), a special train, commencing at Guide Bridge, left Hyde Central at 9.35pm and called to pick up at Woodley, Stockport Tiviot Dale and Northenden before heading for Liverpool Central and a connection with the Isle of Man boat which sailed at 1am in the morning (Douglas arr. 5.50am). For those holidaying in the West Country, a train left Hyde Central at 10.23pm for Stockport Edgeley, with a connecting train making the overnight journey which would see an arrival in (for instance) Torquay at 7.10am; period return fare 102/- (£5.10p). Saturday (13th August) proved busier, with two trains being provided for those with a liking for North Wales. The first, at 8.20am, would again call at Woodley, Stockport T D, and Northenden on its way to (firstly) Prestatyn and stations to Llandudno. The second, at 12.30pm, took another route, this time calling at Hyde North, Guide Bridge, Denton, Reddish South, Stockport Edgeley and Northenden. Prestatyn was once again the first call before proceding to Llandudno. The train (ex. Chinley) taking holidaymakers to Blackpool and the Fylde Coast was timed for 10.52am and called at Hyde North and Guide Bridge, before going forward to Blackpool; the period return fare was 12/6 (62½p). Passengers for Lancaster and Morecambe also used this train but had to change at Preston to reach their destinations. *Reporter Group/courtesy E M Johnson*

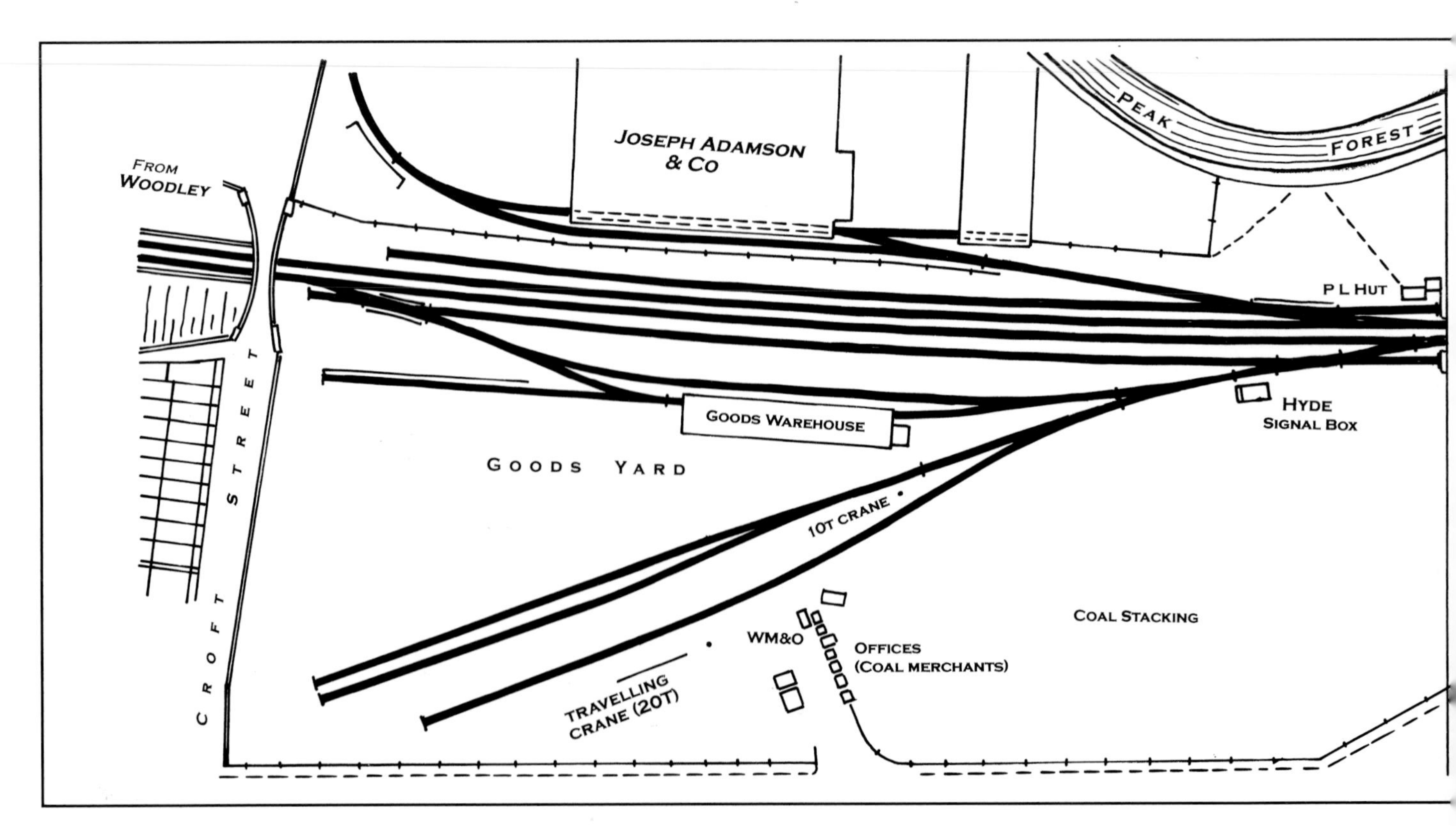

Hyde Central, 23rd September, 1966. The imposing building that faced Great Norbury Street gave perhaps an impression of a station befitting operational facilities on rather a more grand scale than two platforms suggests. The view here shows the 1862 building to the left of the picture, access to and from the platforms being via a subway at the south end of the station. This arrangement was later superseded by the addition of the tall building immediately to the left of the entrance, which was also part of the scheme. Booking and Commercial facilities were just inside the entrance on the right behind extensive wooden panelling. The circulating area beneath the decorative roof lights of the Booking Hall gave access to the 'subway' and several flights of stairs which in turn enabled the passenger to reach the platforms. Last minute passengers were able to produce their own 'hold that train' signal by virtue of the noise generated whilst pounding up the wooden stairs. ***G Biddle***

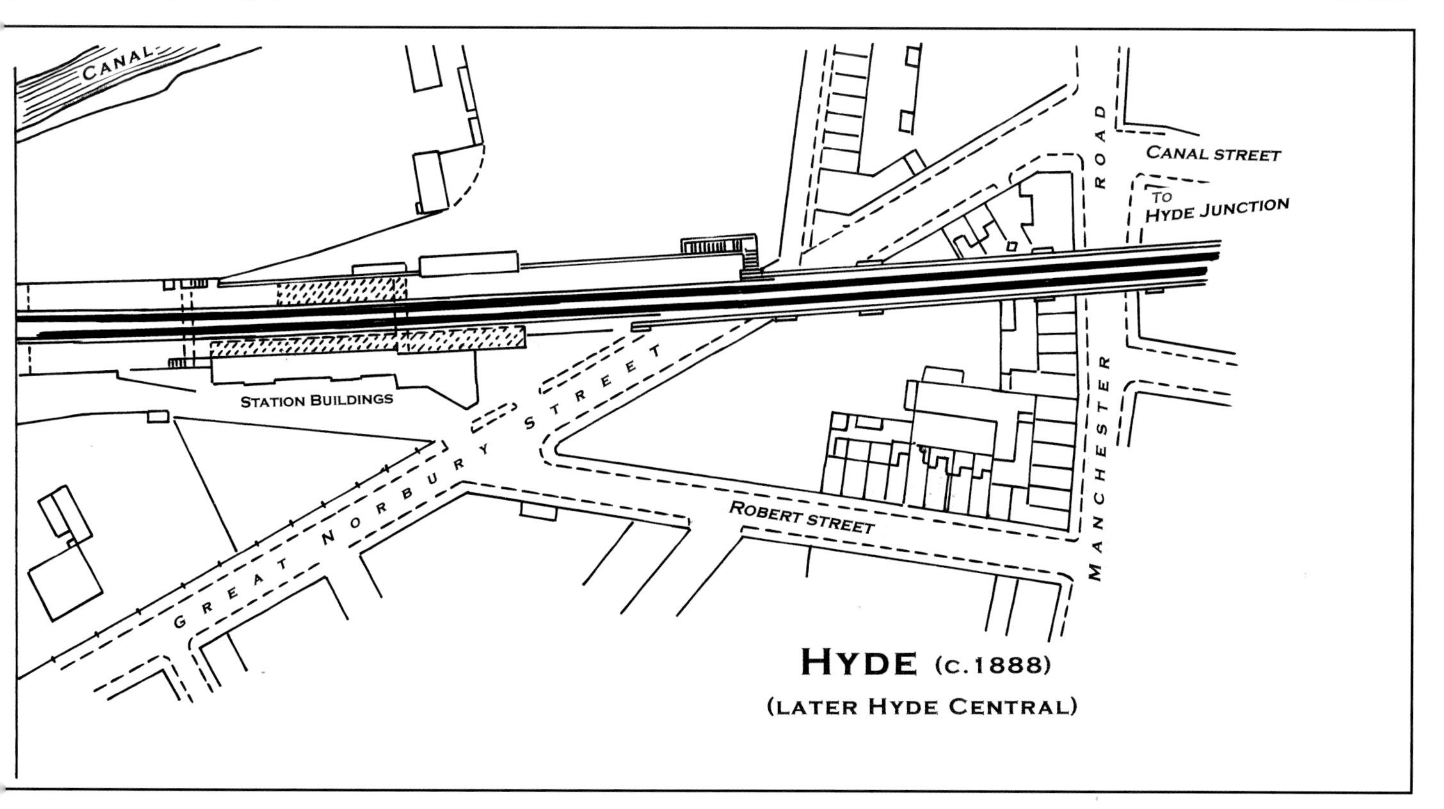

Hyde North, c.1970. The railways had emerged from the 'Beeching' period in a poor state and the cracks were showing, particularly when it came to station infrastructure. There were, as always, limited resources, but they would be aimed at 'rationalisation'. In other words, the traditional railway, with station staffing and comfort from waiting room fires, and the like, would vanish forever. Facilities would be reduced to a bare minimum; open fronted 'bus' style shelters, portable ticket office buildings, etc; As a result, the station buildings here would be razed to the ground, along with the waiting 'room' opposite. A Gloucester RC&W 2-car set (later Class 100) dmu departs for Guide Bridge. ***G K Fox***

(Centre) A view of the main station buildings from the approach adjacent to Junction Street. The facilities were far in excess of the use that was being made of them, a far cry from the early 1950s when eleven and nine coach excursion trains commenced their half day and evening journeys from here. Examples quoted in the RCTS 'Railway Observer' for the period include a mid-day excursion (20th May 1950) to Southport Lord Street, calling at Hyde, Woodley and Stockport Tiviot Dale. Coaching stock incuded a Midland six-coach low-roof close-coupled set and a Midland Clerestory. On 16th July, an evening excursion to Chester and hauled by Trafford Park (9E) Midland 4F No 43896, required nine coaches. Calling at Hyde, Woodley, Stockport, Cheadle, Northenden and Baguley. It was thought that this train was probably the first passenger working (with the exception of troop trains) to traverse the Skelton Junction - Deansgate Junction curve since before WW2. How times have changed ! ***G K Fox***

(Right-lower) Standardisation of buildings by the various railway companies in the 19th Century was commonplace. The MS&L were no exception and here at Hyde North in 1970 on the Up platform is an example of a modular design which was adopted by the GCR and the LNER in its early days. The footpath to Flowery Field is indicated by the 'Way Out' sign. ***G K Fox***

(Right) Serving the industrial district of Dukinfield rather than Hyde itself, Hyde North station, as its name implies, was situated approximately one mile north of the town centre. A footpath from the Up (southbound) platform provided the link with nearby Flowery Field although the building of a new station in 1985 to serve that area did not exactly benefit services on the 'Hyde Loop', as it is known these days. This August 1968 view looking south towards Hyde Central shows a station possessing all of the facilities that were still expected of British Railways. The footbridge was typical of a design originating from the MS&L. ***M A King***

(Centre) Hyde Junction on 7th June 1948 with Class C13 No **67401** at the head of the 5.45pm Manchester London Road to Hadfield train before the Sheffield line was electrified. The station name would be changed in 1951. The background is dominated by the premises of Daniel Adamson & Co; major engineering employers in the area. ***W A Camwell***

(Right) The second Hyde Junction signal box, of Great Central origin and built in conjunction with the quadrupling of the line from Ardwick in 1905/6. The box had a set of 44 levers at the time of the photograph (March 1974) with 31 working. The ground frame serving the Fletcher Miller siding was electrically released from Hyde Junction. The box closed on 14th October 1984. ***M A King***

(Left) A 1967 view of Romiley Junction showing a Metropolitan Cammell 2-car diesel multiple unit heading downhill towards its next stop at Bredbury. The lines on the right have recently closed to traffic (11th August 1967) and the rails are rusting over. Also note that home signal protecting the junction on the Stockport line has had its arm removed. ***Ian R Smith***

ROMILEY

RATIONALISATION

The effects of the Beeching Report resulted in the loss of the services to and from Stockport (Tiviot Dale). At the time the service was fairly sparse and not particularly well patronised. The local bus services provided by the North Western Road Car Company along with Stockport and Manchester Corporations, was more than adequate for districts to the south and east of the town. Four decades on - what would Marple and Romiley residents give for an eleven/seven minute journey to the centre of Stockport ! The two pictures seen here show the last rites of the line between Romiley and Bredbury Junctions. Following closure, the tracks were retained in situ because of "complications" - official terminology - that might occur if the Cheadle Heath to New Mills line closed (as a consequence of road proposals to the south of Stockport). Ultimately, it was decided to lift the disused tracks and this was carried out between May and July 1975. **(Right)** From Quarry Road bridge looking in the direction of Bredbury tunnels, the demolition train stands on the remnants of the former Down line, the Up alignment having already been cleared. **(Below)** With Romiley station to the upper left of the picture, the demolition train pauses on the rump of the closed line in readiness for a return to Moston Ballast Sidings where track components, for which there was a shortage, would be off-loaded and sent to Ditton Sleeper Depot, near Liverpool. Before the journey back to Moston, it was necessary for the locos to position their train on the main line prior to running light to Marple Wharf Junction, where they would cross over. A return to Romiley would enable the run round procedure to be completed. The absence of signal posts and their arms (compare with the view above) can be explained by the fact that the modernisation scheme between Ashburys and Romiley had taken place a couple of years earlier. ***John Fairclough***

(Above-right) The first of three views on this page from Quarry Road bridge, Romiley, shows C13 Class No **67439** coming off the Hyde line with a Hayfield bound train from Manchester London Road. ***T Lewis***

(Centre) This mid-1960s view of an afternoon Manchester Central to Sheffield Midland (via Stockport) train portrays Stanier Class 5MT 4-6-0 No **44708** of Trafford Park (9E) hauling four BR Mark 1 coaches. The signal post to the right of the picture, formerly with a single arm - outer home signal - on the Bredbury line, has received an additional (distant) arm, replacing an older signal located nearer to Bredbury tunnel. Compare this view with those on page 45, and note also that the more heavily used Bredbury lines have been relaid using flat bottom rail. ***John Fairclough***

Romiley Junction, 31st May 1966. 'Jubilee' Class 6P5F 4-6-0 No **45581** *Bihar and Orissa* hauls the empty stock for a return Belle Vue – West Riding excursion from New Mills South Goods Yard where it had been stored all day. The locomotive had been serviced at Heaton Mersey shed. Romiley Station can be seen to the rear of the train. The declining fortunes of the railway system were now becoming more apparent, with the small goods yard, closed from 30th January 1965, having been removed quite hastily to add to the growing acreage of derelict railway infrastructure. ***Ian R Smith***

BUILT NORTH BRITISH LOCO 1934. W/DRN 8/1966. KINGMOOR 1937, 1942 AND 1948

(Above) Romiley, 2nd October 1964. Coming off the Hyde line, Stanier 8F No **48261** of Buxton shed, running light engine from Godley, approaches the junction at Romiley on its way back to base. A member of the train crew, armed with camera, has given us this splendid rail level view of all three routes merging to form the line south to Marple and New Mills. To the left we have the 1 in 71 climb from Bredbury Junction. The middle route from Reddish, rising at a more modest 1 in 91 is encountered on the right by the route from Hyde, with its leisurely 1 mile ascent from Woodley Junction. ***J M Bentley***

(Right-centre) On 22nd September 1961 the preserved Great Central Class D11E 4-4-0 No **565** *Butler Henderson* was towed to Romiley for an official photograph session from Gorton Works where it had been restored following withdrawal from BR service as Class D11/1 No 62660. It is seen in a conspicuously empty goods yard at a time also when the hillside beyond was awaiting the onset of housing development that would change the Romiley landscape forever. This locomotive is now part of the National Railway Collection. ***BR/OPC***

(Right-lower) Throughout the 1950s and '60s, buses continued to play an integral part in local transport. The geography of the region however gave rail the advantage over road as far as travel from and to Manchester was concerned. The No. 83 service (Stockport - Mellor) provided an ideal connection with rail at Romiley for both Compstall and parts of Marple Bridge. About to commence its outward journey from Mersey Square is a North Western Road Car Company Bristol K5G, re-built in 1952 with a Willowbrook 'lowbridge' body on a 1939 chassis. Users of these buses may well remember the cramped upstairs conditions, a result of the low headroom and long single seats intended for four passengers. ***Photobus***

 NO 459 ORIG BODIED BY ECW L23/24R, REBODIED AS SEEN W'BROOK L27/26R

Romiley, 15th March 1952. Class C14 4-4-2T No **67448** rolls alongside the Up platform with a train bound for Macclesfield Central, having come from London Road via Reddish. A present day feature of the station is the signal box, a Midland Railway structure of 1899 which originally had a 36-lever frame and was a replacement for an earlier box. The station still had a healthy volume of domestic coal traffic, although the goods yard, with only a capacity for 31wagons, was fairly cramped. ***J D Darby***

(Right-lower) Romiley station looking north at platform level on 1st August 1963. The wooden sections of platform were integral with the bridge (No 33 on the Hayfield to Woodley line) that carried the railway across Romiley's main thoroughfare, Stockport Road. Access to the station was at street level, requiring three flights of stairs, contained within an attractive octagonal building surmounted by a glazed cupola, to reach the Down, or Manchester bound platform. The Booking Office and Hall were on the second floor adjacent to a subway which connected with the Up platform. The subway had been added in 1891 when the platforms were lengthened. The platform buildings on the Up side, with distinct MS&L features, were also added at this time. Bridge No 33 was reconstructed in 1895 to complete the station more or less as we know it today. Cast iron lamp standards with gas lighting, and signal posts (albeit with LMS upper quadrant arms) along with a Midland signal box give a feel for the early years of the station. The disc signal in between the lines controlled the crossover which occasionally enabled wrong line working when engineers were in possession of the line. ***P E Baughan***

ROMILEY

A commercial postcard view from the 1950s of the 'west' end of Romiley looking along Stockport Road from a point adjacent to the Romiley Arms. Romiley station is to the right, the entrance immediately to the right of the newsagents kiosk at road level. On the second floor is the Booking Office and entrance to the subway (Br.33A) for the Up platform. Another flight of stairs is required to reach the Down (northbound) platform. The scene is still recognisable with that of today, save for the pram, car, kiosk and concrete bus shelter. The impressive facade of the original station building overlooks the footpath to the right of the kiosk. The glazed cupola set in the roof of the high red-bricked extension highlights the extension to the station completed in 1892. Reconstruction of Stockport Road bridge took place in 1895 and allowed for the platforms to be extended across the bridge, the steelwork being provided by the Derby firm of Andrew Handyside. It is still possible to see the manufacturers plate on the girders of the bridge. This extra work also entailed the building of the substantial stone retaining wall seen here, above which the words 'Railway Station' appear, set in relief in the parapet wall. In recent years, cleaning of the station exterior has also revealed the attractive terra-cotta mouldings above the entrance.

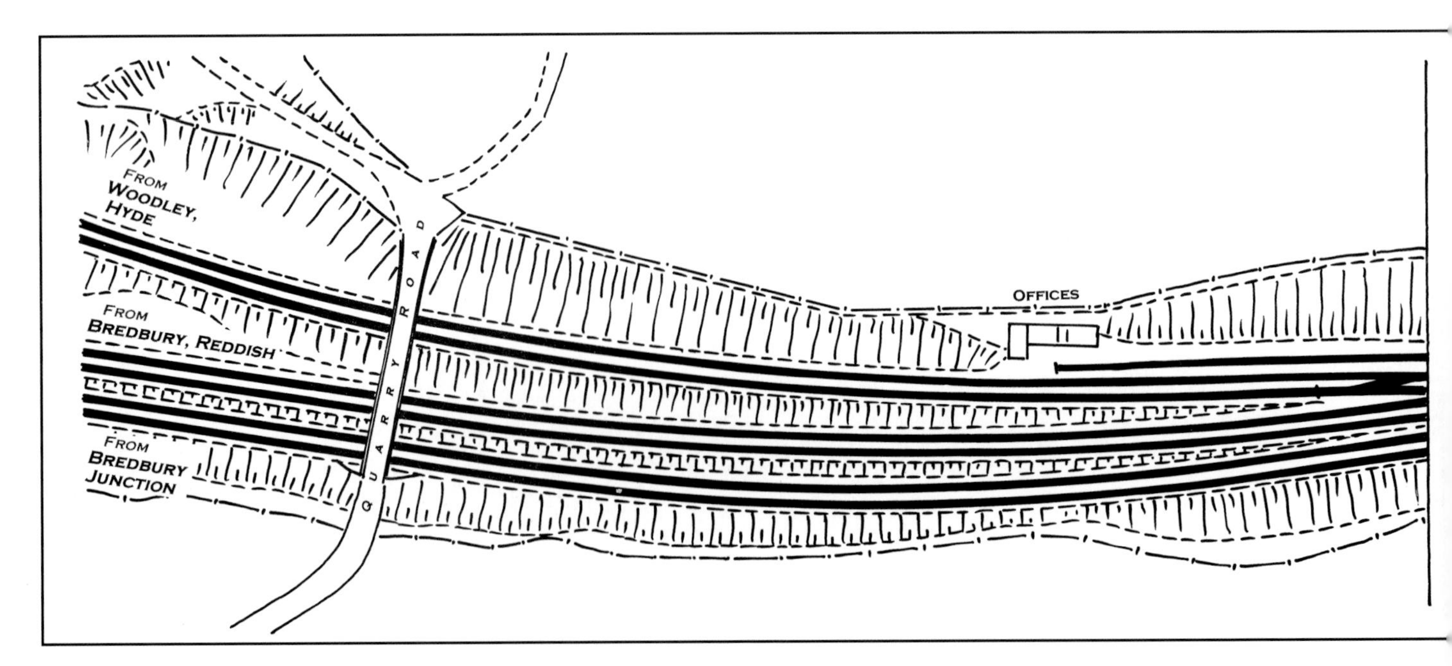

(Right) Setting off from Romiley. The driver and fireman of this unidentified Stanier 2-6-0 look back as they get their train moving downhill towards Marple. Arriving in the opposite direction is a four car diesel multiple unit bound for Manchester Piccadilly. It comprises an original Derby Lightweight plus three Metropolitan Cammell cars. The use of Stanier 2-6-0s on the line was unusual until Gorton received an allocation circa 1965. They were then used on the morning and evening steam services from Manchester Piccadilly to Hayfield and it is likely that this is one such working, the 17.30 from Piccadilly. ***John Fairclough***

(Above) Below platform level at Romiley on the Compstall Road/ Guywood Lane side of the bridge, adjacent the road entrance to the goods yard, stood this wooden sectional building which housed the Romiley District office of the Derby North Signal and Telegraph Engineers. Made of Midland Railway signal box components, it provided accommodation for the staff who maintained the relevant equipment between Romiley and Millers Dale. Reorganisation of the LM engineering functions in 1966 saw an end to this arrangement and maintenance passed over to a newly formed Manchester Division. ***Graham Whitehead***

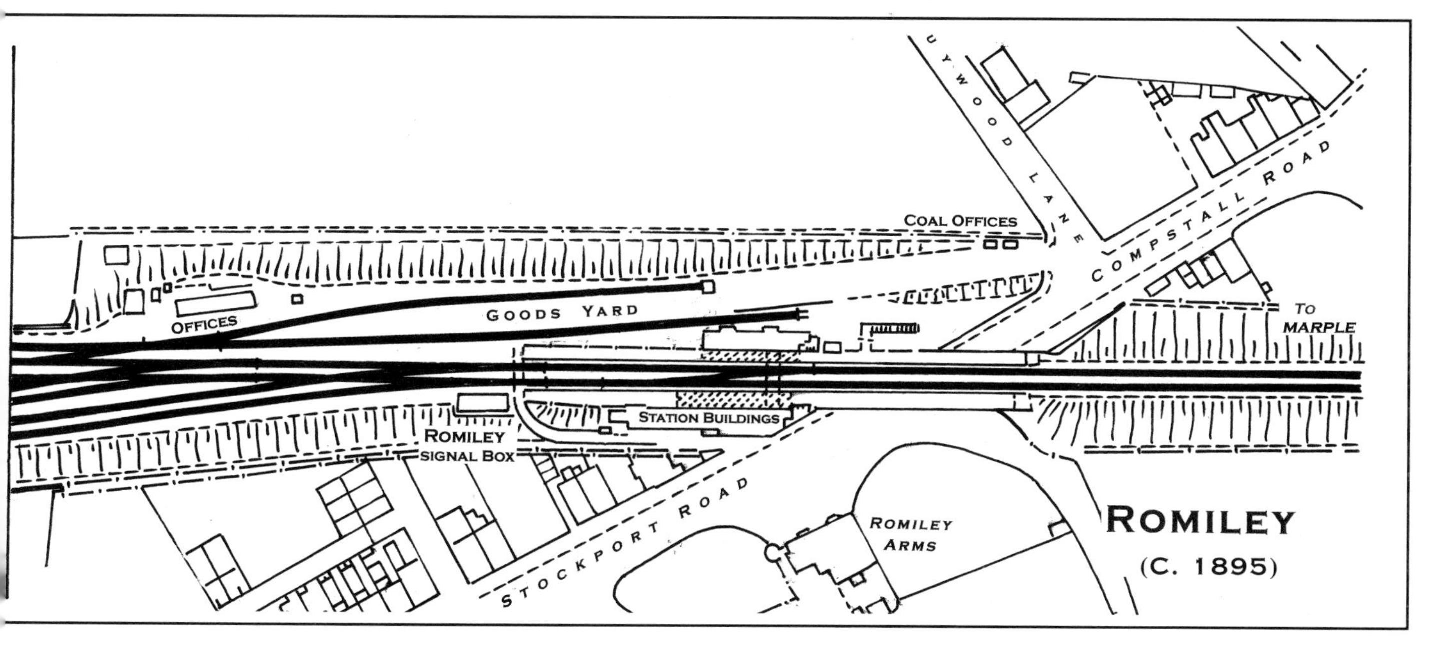

An old photographic postcard view of Romiley, looking south, possibly taken around 1910, but most certainly before 1920 when bridge No 59 (Vaudreys) - right hand side of picture - was removed and the opening filled in. A continuation of what is now Hill Street, this occupation bridge had a chequered life, initially being constructed for the original (1861) Hayfield -Woodley line and being extended in 1874 for the Reddish and Bredbury lines. Ironically, it was partially reconstructed in 1912, only eight years before removal. A passenger train appears to be coming off the Reddish line as the engine enters the station.There is a goods yard full of coal wagons in a landscape that would remain largely unchanged until the 1960s when development of the land in the foreground blocked the view from the point above Quarry Road. Landmarks include the chimney to Oakwood Mills - into which a private siding was proposed as late as 1953 - and the spire of the Parish Church of St Chads in Church Lane. ***Mrs J Fox collection***

(Left) On 18th April 1954, Romiley Station northbound platform is viewed from a southbound train. This has come from Manchester Central and caused a goods train to wait on the Reddish line in the distance. The Midland Railway wooden framed station sign was soon to be replaced by a maroon BR metal sign. ***H C Casserley***

(Below-left) An afternoon Manchester Central – Sheffield Midland stopping train stops at Romiley on 1st February 1964. The use of 'Peak' (Class 45) diesel electric No **D106** on what was usually a three coach stopping train was a fill-in turn between express duties at Manchester. The 16C shed plate indicated that the locomotive belonged to Derby. The train is steam heated (most diesel locomotives at that time had a steam boiler for this purpose) and the tell-tale leaks below the locomotive and between the carriages show this. ***Graham Whitehead***

'Peak' Class 45 diesel electric locomotive No **D55** heads a mixed goods train northbound through Romiley on 1st February 1964. ***Graham Whitehead***

(Above) Romiley, August 1966. Late afternoon brings a short flurry of activity to the station as the 15.30 Manchester Central to Sheffield train runs alongside the Up platform with Trafford Park (9E) based Stanier Class 5 4-6-0 No **44851** providing the motive power. This view in the direction of Manchester shows a station that has seen numerous changes, albeit of a minor nature, but which have not altered the overall effect. The decorative cupola above the stair well on the left has long since gone, along with the iron lamp standards with their gas fittings along the platforms. Passengers will lament the loss of the toilet facilities, although the outside gents urinals were frequently out of use when frozen up in the winter months. The most obvious change is to the signalling which has seen replacement of the once dominant semaphores with colour light counterparts.

(Centre) 'Black Five' No **44851** waits to depart (16.02) from Romiley on a journey which is due to take 112 minutes for the 46¾ miles between Manchester and Sheffield Midland station.

(Right-lower) The photographer used the service on a regular basis and recalls that a freight train ran through the station on the Down line whilst he was alighting. On this occasion however, he was able to record this daily occurrance from the Marple end of the Down (Manchester bound) platform as Class 5 No **44890**, a long time resident of Newton Heath (9D) depot, approaches from the Marple direction.

All; ***Adrian Rowlands***

Romiley-Oakwood. A smart-looking Class C14 4-4-2T No **67447** heads south from Romiley down the bank at Oakwood towards Marple Wharf Junction in 1951. The train was approaching the site of the one-time Oakwood Signal Box, an early casualty to rationalisation when its functions were transferred between Marple Wharf and Romiley Junction boxes in 1933. The train is a Manchester (London Road) to Macclesfield Central via Hyde working. The first and third coaches are of Great Central origin, the second coach is North Eastern and the fourth coach is a Gresley design for the LNER. The last coach is a turn of the century clerestory coach of MS&L construction. In 1951 this C14 would have been fairly new to the line, having been latterly working in Yorkshire. Originally constructed for the London suburban services out of Marylebone the locomotive was already forty years old when it arrived at Gorton *.Eric Oldham*

Romiley-Oakwood. Taking advantage of the downhill stretch - 1 in 150 - having 'slogged' its way to Romiley from Stockport (Tiviot Dale), a local stopping train from Manchester Central is seen approaching Oakwood between Romiley and Marple. This view, taken about 1951, shows the train being hauled by a class of locomotive destined to see out steam on the line; the Stanier Class 5 4-6-0. **45264** was a Millhouses (Sheffield - 19B) engine until 1952 before being dispatched to serve various East Midlands depots. It looks as if it may have been on a running in turn following overhaul at Derby Works. The stock is painted in the 'carmine and cream' livery used for main line vehicles in the early part of the 1950s. Sometimes referred to as 'blood and custard', it was an attractive livery but in days of limited cleaning facilities was soon superseded - on all regions - by more practical, if drab, colour schemes. Above the tender of the loco is one of the local landmarks, Top 'o' th Hill, a large flat topped building which dominates the landscape above Romiley and the surrounding districts. *Eric Oldham*

(Left) Oakwood, c. 1966. Although not of the highest quality, this view of an unidentified Class 5 on a Sheffield bound train is included to illustrate Romiley Junction's Up intermediate block home signal that was formerly the Oakwood signal box (Closed 18th June 1933) Up home. This wooden posted signal was replaced in September 1976 by a tubular steel version.

Adrian Rowlands

2nd - SINGLE SINGLE - 2nd

9620

Marple To

Marple Romiley | Marple Romiley

ROMILEY

(M) 0/4 Fare 0/4 (M)

For conditions see over For conditions see over

(Right) Having just cleared Oakwood Bridge (No 31 - known originally as Wood's bridge) between Romiley and Marple Wharf Junction, the driver of Class C13 4-4-2T No **67415** appears to be preparing for the long climb from Marple to New Mills. This 1952 view of a Manchester (London Road) to Hayfield train shows the safety valves lifting as black smoke indicates coal being applied. The train is passing the site of Oakwood Signal Box - note the dark inclined retaining wall to the left, whilst above the engine to the right would spring the Cherry Tree housing development of the late 1950s. Approaching its fiftieth year in service, this Gorton veteran was withdrawn in February 1956. ***Eric Oldham***

(Right-centre) In 1950, a Fowler designed 2-6-4T No **42356** (Macclesfield - 9C) is seen climbing from Marple Wharf Junction towards Romiley. Although it bears its new BR number on the front and side, its side tank still proclaims LMS ownership. This light-weight goods train would have originated from the North Staffordshire section at Macclesfield, whose shed provided locomotives for this goods service as well as the local trains on the ex-LNWR route from Macclesfield (Hibel Road) to Manchester (London Road). The concrete structure, hidden partially behind the loco's chimney, was known locally as the 'Giants Table' and was a well-known landmark along the line. It was the shell of a former brickworks and more recently a wartime defence post. It was a favourite play spot for local children from the nearby Cherry Tree estate. Its unexpected demolition, on a safety issue, caused uproar amongst generations of Romiley folk who had come to regard the structure with affection. ***Eric Oldham***

(Right-lower) Moving on a decade at the same location as above (centre). The Derby Lightweight unit has lost its 'speed whiskers' on the front to be replaced by a small rectangular yellow warning panel. The distinctive and attractive front end of these diesels did not suffer greatly by this change although the comparative shortness of life of the 'Lightweights' meant that few would be endowed with the all-over yellow ends. ***G K Fox***

(Left) Approaching what is thought to have been the site of Compstall station, used until the valley had been spanned by Marple Viaduct, is the empty stock of a West Riding to Belle Vue Bank Holiday excursion on 11th April 1966. It was hauled, unusually for the time, by a Brush (BR Crewe-built) Type 4 No **D1551.** At the time this locomotive, subsequently Class 47 (Tops No 47 529), would have been front line motive power for the East Coast Main Line and had only left Crewe as a new locomotive in January 1964. The Peak Forest Canal, never very far away, is down the field to the left, but a short distance away. ***Ian R Smith***

Three years earlier at the same spot as above, a Derby Lightweight 2-car set hurries downhill towards Marple Wharf Junction. The one and three-quarter mile section between Romiley and Marple provided an opportunity on the outward journey for a spell of fast running, an average of four minutes being allowed between stations. In the top right of the picture, the houses on Hydebank mark the point at which the Peak Forest Canal tunnels beneath the hillside. ***G K Fox***

(Right) Passing Romiley's Cherry Tree Estate, adjacent to the site of Oakwood Signal Box, the 15.00 Manchester (Piccadilly) to Hayfield via Reddish rattles downhill towards Marple Wharf Junction on 29th January 1966. Comprising a two car 'Original' Derby Lightweight set and a two car Metropolitan-Cammell set, these early design units (Yellow Diamond) were incompatible with multiple units on many other routes and thus these local lines south and east of Manchester tended to retain these incongruous units until they too succumbed only a couple of years after this photo was taken. ***Ian R Smith***

(Left) A long goods train toils up the 1 in 150 grade from Marple Viaduct towards Romiley behind LMS built Class 5 4-6-0 No **44871** on 29th January 1966. Unusually for this line, the locomotive was based at Stockport (Edgeley). The train is a Gowhole to Dewsnap (near Guide Bridge) working, at the end of which the locomotive could be conveniently positioned for return to its home shed. Despite the ongoing reduction in demand for local freight workings, there was still a daily local trip working from Stockport to Dewsnap which might explain the above situation. ***Ian R Smith***

(Above) Marple Viaduct, c.1956. A5 Class 4-6-2T No **69828** is seen here crossing Marple Viaduct and heading towards Romiley. Having just come off the Macclesfield line and endured a 15mph speed restriction due to the tight curve, this Manchester bound train will be faced with a 1 1/4 mile climb at 1 in 150 before its Romiley stop. Beyond the last carriage can be seen the signal box and signals which controlled movements at Marple Wharf Junction. ***W A Brown***

(Right-lower) LMS built 4P (3-cyl Compound) 4-4-0 No **41079** drifts south across Marple Viaduct with a Manchester (Central) to Chinley train in 1950, although being a Millhouses (19B) engine suggests that the train would continue to Sheffield. The driver is leaning out on the fireman's side, peering intently towards Marple Wharf Junction, whilst the safety valves have lifted indicating a good head of steam for the long climb ahead. The repairs above arches 11 and 12 of the viaduct, made in brick during the 1930s, have left a permanent mark on this otherwise fine structure. ***Eric Oldham***

Marple Viaduct as seen from the north west around 1900. A train of 14 carriages of both four and six wheeled varieties crosses the viaduct heading towards Marple. The locomotive is a saddle tank, possibly an MS&L 0-6-0ST of Class 18T, constructed at Gorton in 1880. The carriages are in both MS&L and GCR liveries. The signal box and signals were originally installed and maintained by the MS&LR, although maintenance of these early installations was taken over by the Midland Railway in 1876. The signal box was replaced by a Midland pattern wooden structure in 1927. The new box, with a 20-lever tappet frame, was sited nearer to the viaduct. In the foreground is the spectacular aqueduct carrying the Peak Forest Canal over the Goyt before passing under the steel skew bridge which formed the first of the fourteen openings of Marple Viaduct. To the right of the picture is the long established works which occupied a cliff top position at the south end of the aqueduct. Telegraph wires for the railway were carried across the aqueduct, an arrangement much simplified by the ownership of the Peak Forest Canal by the Great Central Railway. ***Warwick Burton collection***

Marple Viaduct across the valley of the River Goyt is the scene for a two car Birmingham RCW (Class 104) DMU working the 14.30 Marple – Manchester Piccadilly train on 2nd April 1968. In the foreground is Outram's magnificent canal viaduct, fortunately having been restored following the potentially catastrophic partial collapse of the early 1960s, carrying the Peak Forest Canal over the valley. This canal was bought by the MS&LR in an attempt to gain a foothold in the area years before the railway could follow. ***Ian R Smith***

(Right) Crossing Marple Viaduct on 22nd April 1966, Class 5MT 4-6-0 No **45073** catches the evening sunlight whilst hauling the 17.30 Sheffield Midland–Manchester Central train.In the left foreground are the still waters of the Peak Forest Canal. Strengthening of the viaduct in the 1930s by concreting shortened lengths of rail into and above the arch rings resulted in the use of bricks rather than stone to repair the spandrels. They stand out as they reflect the sunshine. ***Ian R Smith***

(Right-centre) Marple Viaduct on 30th May 1967. A four car diesel multiple unit set speeds its way across the viaduct with a Manchester (Piccadilly) to Hayfield train whilst Stanier Class 5 4-6-0 No **45001** lifts the empty stock of a returning Belle Vue to Bradford train up the gradient towards Romiley. The DMU comprises a two car Derby 'Original' Lightweight set (furthest from the camera) and a Metropolitan Cammell two car set. The brickwork on the Up side face resulting from the strengthening process described above can be seen clearly beneath the locomotive. In contrast to the turn of the century view, the Aqueduct Works has spread across the site somewhat and now appears as low manufacturing sheds. To the left and rear of the excursion train is Marple Wharf Junction signal box. ***Ian R Smith***

(Below) Marple Viaduct seen from the canal aqueduct on 31st May 1966. On the right the buildings of the Aqueduct Works, extensively rebuilt in the early years of the twentieth century look decidedly unkempt although the aqueduct itself is looking in good condition following its extensive rebuilding just a few years before the photograph was taken. In this late evening shot, Class 6P5F 4-6-0 No **45647** *Sturdee* is returning the empty stock of a Whit Monday excursion to Belle Vue where it will collect returning passengers for the West Riding. At the time, No **45647** was one of the dwindling survivors of the LMS built 'Jubilee' Class. Although rare on this route by 1966, this locomotive and No **45581** both appeared hauling specials on the same day. This photograph is a reminder of days when 'Jubilee' 4-6-0 locomotives were more common on Midland line trains over this route, particularly the afternoon Liverpool to Nottingham service. ***Ian R Smith***

(Above) Viewed from rail level of the Macclesfield lines, LNER designed (Vulcan-built 1947) B1 Class 4-6-0 No **61161** crosses the junction at at Marple Wharf with the empty stock of a West Riding to Belle Vue excursion on 15th April 1963. The train would continue to New Mills South Goods Yard to be stored until evening whilst the locomotive made its way to Heaton Mersey for servicing. **61161** was a Wakefield engine and this probably indicates the area from which the excursion originated. The stock is a mixture of LMS and LNER built suburban stock. On such a long run without a corridor (and access to toilets) the discomfort of some of the passengers can be imagined. ***Locofotos***

(Right-centre) Signalman's view of the 16.20 Manchester (Piccadilly) to Hayfield (via Hyde) as it passes Marple Wharf Junction on 17th April 1966. The train has just crossed the skew bridge (reconstructed in this form 1907) carrying the railway over the Peak Forest Canal at the south end of Marple Viaduct. On the left the Aqueduct works is just visible. ***Ian R Smith***

(Right-lower) Marple Wharf Junction, c. 1952. From the end of the viaduct the severe curve of the Macclesfield line is not exaggerated and the reason for a 15mph restriction can clearly be seen. The box had a 20 lever frame and closed on the 27th July 1980 following re-signalling between Romiley and New Mills. It is just south of here where some four miles of adverse gradients commence, nominally at 1 in 100, checked occasionally by level spells at Marple station and Goyt Cliff Viaduct. ***Scrimgoer collection/SRS***

(Left) Following the closure of Manchester (Central) but before the abandonment of the line through Millers Dale and Bakewell, a semi-fast service operated from Manchester (Piccadilly) to Nottingham (Midland), stopping at Chinley, Matlock and Derby. Usually formed of a two car Cravens DMU (later Class 105), they travelled at maximum line speed over much of the route. Seen here crossing the Peak Forest Canal at Marple Wharf Junction on 2nd April 1968, the 14.15 Manchester to Nottingham train is formed of a Cravens set, the first vehicle of which is in the overall BR blue with yellow front, whilst the second coach is still in lined green livery. ***Ian R Smith***

(Below) Marple Wharf Junction on 30th May 1967. The empty stock of a returning Belle Vue to Leeds excursion clatters across the junction behind Class 5 4-6-0 No **44897**, recently a Birkenhead (8H) based engine but here running without a shed plate. Within months it would be allocated to Carnforth to see out its time before withdrawal in August 1968. The Macclesfield line, seen here bearing off to the right, had a very tight curvature which necessitated the use of check rails commencing at the junction. Marple Wharf Junction also marked the boundary between the Derby North and Stoke Districts. A square, white painted post, is seen on the extreme right of the picture at the bottom of page 74 with the respective names. The short spur to Marple Wharf left the main line to the left just behind the locomotive, although the site of this long removed connection can still be identified by a shallow cutting. ***Ian R Smith***

MARPLE WHARF JUNCTION

(Left) Class G2a 0-8-0 No **49093** waits at Marple Wha Junction in August 1956. The tall Midlan signal was soon to be replaced by a smaller BI tubular steel structure placed near to where th photographer was standing. The train was being held t enable a passenger working to leave the Macclesfiel line. Meanwhile, one of the numerous WD Class 2-8-0 is seen heading in the opposite direction, possibly with train of empty coal wagons from either Ellesmere Port o Middleton Junction. There were also similar trains fron places such as Dundas Sidings, Garston, etc., with a lis of destinations reading Carlton, Staveley, Roundwooc Wincobank, Grimesthorpe, to name but a few. It reall was a "conveyor-belt" serving the coal industry. Withi a decade, scenes such as this would vanish. The prestig working of the weekday traffic would undoubtedly hav been the Somers Town (St Pancras) to Ancoats whicl ran during the early hours. The sixty or so daily freigh trains booked over this section of line would be reduce to less than ten. ***Eric Oldhan***

(Right) Having been held at the junction, No **49093,** carrying an 8B shed plate, bursts into life as it tackles the uphill gradient to Romiley. The train, photographed in August 1956, is a loose-coupled mixture of wooden-bodied and the then - new BR 16 ton mineral wagons. Engine crews of trains approaching Marple Wharf Junction from the Down (New Mills) direction, were required to indicate their intended route (at Romiley) - via Stockport or Woodley - in the form of engine whistles, one long and one short for Stockport, one long and two short for Woodley. The train seen here, although not specifically identified, could quite easily have been the Codnor Park to Heaton Mersey working. Destinations for Down trains were as diverse as Ancoats, Ashton Road, Brewery Sidings, Brindle Heath, Collyhurst Street, Heysham, Liverpool, Portwood (Stockport), Stuart Street,etc., "Super Ds", as these LNWR stalwarts were popularly known, were not overly frequent visitors to the line. ***Eric Oldham***

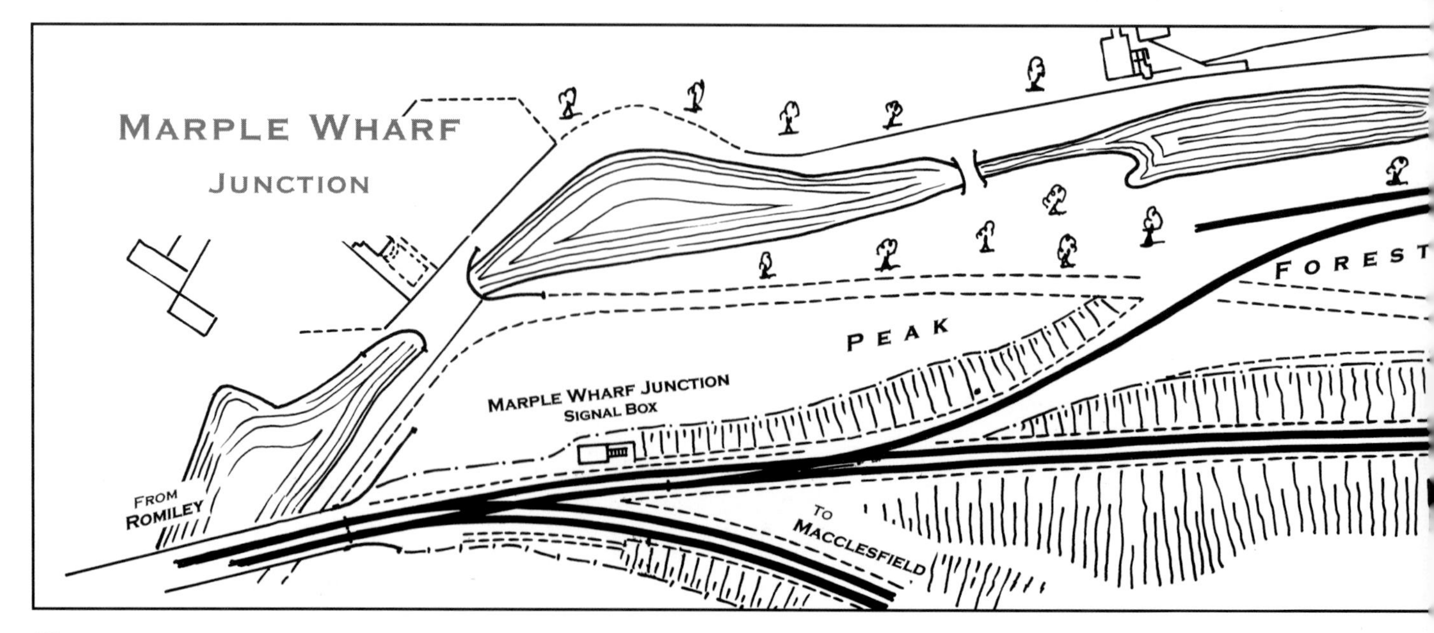

(Left) Heading towards Marple North Tunnel; Br No 29 - 99 yards (90 metres) - with Marple Wharf Junction in the background, the 10.00 Manchester Piccadilly to Sheffield Midland train is about to pass under the Peak Forest Canal on 8th April 1968. The canal, with its sixteen consecutive locks, passes beneath the railway just beyond the signal box, yet is above it at the point where the photographer is standing, a little more than a quarter of a mile away. The train is formed of an Eastern Region 2 - car dmu and is operating a short-lived hybrid service occasioned by the closure of Manchester Central. The service ran non-stop from Manchester to Chinley following the closure of the route through Stockport Tiviot Dale, after which it picked up its duties as the local train through the Hope Valley to Sheffield. ***Ian R Smith***

Right) Leaving Marple North Tunnel, or 'Marple Canal Arching" as the early Sheffield & ⁄idland authorities identified the structure, Class ⁆14 4-4-2T No **67448** comfortably controls its rain over the last few yards of the falling 1 in 100 gradient before the one and a half mile climb owards Romiley on 24th May 1957. This early fternoon working, the 2.15pm from Marple to Manchester London Road, calling all stations Ardwick excepted) via Hyde, would take a eisurely thirty-five minutes for the journey. What s surprising however, and would undoubtedly provide todays transport protagonists with plenty of ammunition, is the fact that this was the first Monday to Friday train since 10.46 in the norning to cater for the same route. There was a Saturdays Only service for shoppers departing Marple at 12.20 which had come through from Hayfield. To the left of the locomotive - on the Up side - is the 177 Milepost indicating the distance from London St Pancras. The structures however; bridges, tunnels, culverts, etc., were - and still are numbered from Hayfield as far as Woodley, an anachronism which dates back to the Marple, New Mills and Hayfield days. ***W A Brown***

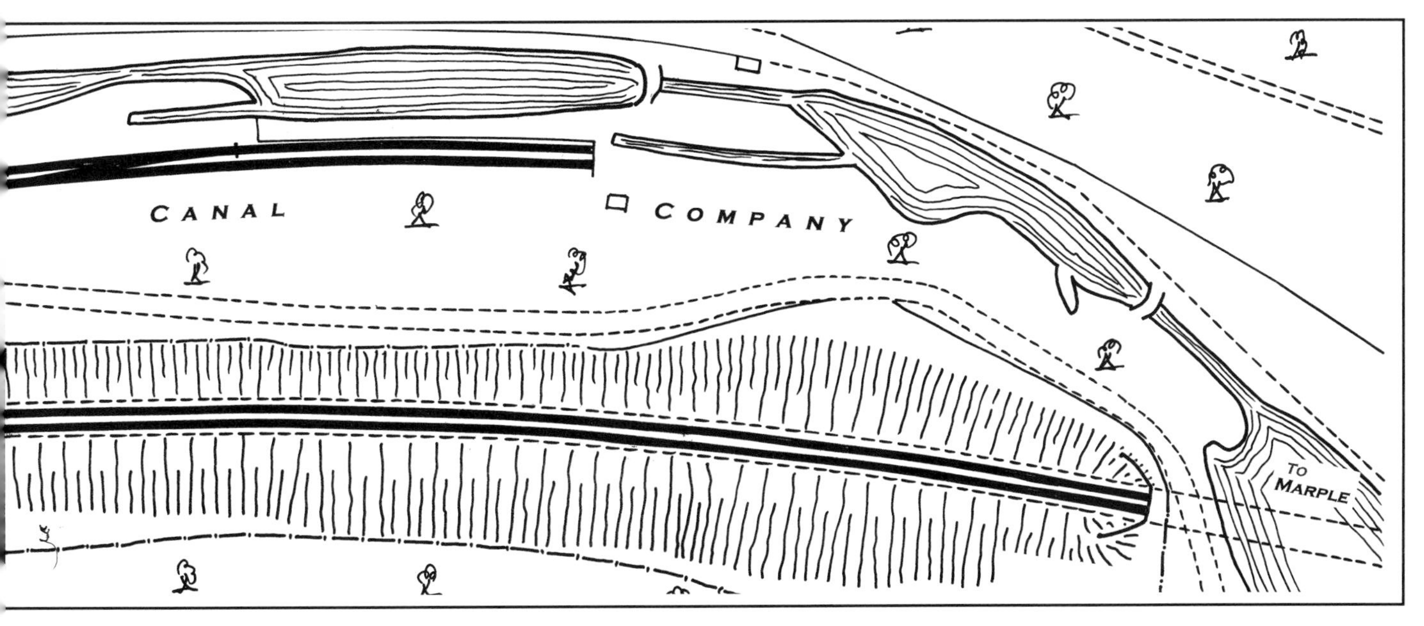

(Right) The weekday departures on the Hayfield route via Reddish, following introduction of diesel multiple units in 1957, were generally on the hour for Hayfield and half past the hour turning back at Marple. The 11.30 Manchester (Piccadilly) to Marple has already had its indicator blind rewound for its return journey as it bursts out of Marple North Tunnel on the last half mile or so of its journey. The date is 31st March 1966 and the train is formed of one of the Derby 'lightweight (79xxx series) diesel multiple units. The tunnel carries the Peak Forest Canal over the line. The heavily blackened board to the right of the tunnel mouth displayed that the tunnel was 99 yards long, but was confusing in that someone had made it look like 199 yards! ***Ian R Smith***

(Centre) Trailing a long train of empty coal wagons, BR Sulzer Type 2 (later Class 25) No **D5281** clears Marple North Tunnel on 8th April 1968. It was on a working from Dewsnap Yard (near Guide Bridge) to Gowhole. The BR tubular post upper quadrant signal protects Marple Station and is giving the train a clear run at the varied adverse gradients that will be encountered beyond Marple station. ***Ian R Smith***

(Below) A four car DMU passes through Brabyns Park on the approach to Marple Station. Leading the 13.00 Manchester Piccadilly – Hayfield train on 14th May 1966 is a Metropolitan Cammell 'yellow diamond' car, followed by three Derby Lightweight vehicles. In the background is Marple North Tunnel. The track formation shows signs of recent disturbance due to the removal of the Marple north end crossover in 1965 and replacement with plain line. ***Ian R Smith***

Above) Marple, 6th April 1957. Approaching the last few yards of its Saturdays Only trip from Manchester, Gorton (39A) based C13 No **67417** finds he slight climb from Marple North tunnel no obstacle at all, the sanctuary of the level section through Marple but a short distance away. Viewed from Iudsons bridge (No28) immediately to the north of the station - see below - the train had left London Road at 1.30pm, Belle Vue being the first stop n its twenty five minute journey via Reddish. In the days when only Marple had a swimming baths to serve the locality, this train was popular with oungsters of Bredbury and Romiley who were quite happy to pay the four (old) pence return fare for the privilege. ***W A Brown***

Right-lower) B1 4-6-0 No **61051** North British Loco built 1946 to NER design) heads the 08.35 train or Manchester Central (ex-Sheffield Midland) out of Marple in December 964. The decommissioned crossover erving the Up Loop (and platform) is isible as is the trolley used for such vork; the Up Loop and Down Bay ines had been removed in October. ust beyond the bridge to the right of he pointwork was the site of the ormer Marple North signal box, one f two originally serving Marple - the ther was Marple South - before eplacement in March 1905 by the ingle structure on the Up platform. By ow the old order in motive power erms had gone and it was Canklow lepot (41D) that operated half of the heffield workings whilst Trafford ark provided motive power for the est. ***Ian R Smith***

Marple, 24th May 1957. The term 'classic' is often misused, but on this occasion it is most certainly justified for this scene viewed from Hudsons bridge at the north end of the station. Marple had changed little in some fifty years, the 'modern' signalling being the chief alteration. Class A5 No **69815**, a comparative newcomer to the area, is still part of the vintage aspect as it leaves with the 1.59 (ex-Hayfield) to Manchester London Road via Reddish. In the Down bay is C14 No **67448** waiting patiently with the stock of the 2.15pm Marple to London Road via Hyde. ***W A Brown***

MARPLE

(Right-lower) Marple Station in the 1950s, viewed from the Up (southbound) platform. The station had been repainted in London Midland Region colours of maroon and cream. The awnings are supported by cast iron work with elegant circular S&M monograms worked into the brackets. The glasswork is still blacked out as a result of the restrictions of the Second World War. At the north end of the opposite (Down) platform a water crane is visible, with another also available in the Bay platform. The wooden-decked footbridge (No 27) was covered and clad with timber. It is the framework of this structure that was retained and serves the station to this day. The wooden building under the bridge on the northbound platform was a store room.

(Above) A view of Marple Station looking south around 1900 presents a very tidy appearance. The Up Loop on the left served both the platform and he goods yard, where the roof of the goods shed is just visible above the platform canopy. Trains from Manchester that terminated at Marple would eturn from either the Up Loop platform or the Down bay platform (on the right) in order to keep them out of the way of the busy through traffic. Train novements were still controlled from two signal boxes located at the extremities of the station *(see station layout on pages 82/83)*. Milk churns are laced adjacent to the platform edge in the Up Loop, presumably convenient for the brake van compartments on arriving trains. The siding on the xtreme left was rarely used, although protecting a headshunt to the goods yard would be its main function. However, there was an instance in 1955 vhen it was used to stable a C14 Class 4-4-2T No 67441 which had failed in service. Although not visible in this view, the $176\frac{3}{4}$ milepost, a cast iron late, was mounted flush on the retaining wall to the left, due to the limited clearance in the cess.

)ne of the impressive 'Crab' Class 5MT 2-6-0s, No **42722** of ower Darwen (10H) shed, powers a Dewsnap–Gowhole oods train through Marple Station on 8th February 1964. The verbridge (No 28) carried the drive for the old Brabyns Hall cross the railway after the line had bisected the parkland.
Graham Whitehead

Marple Signal Box looking north on 8th February 1964. It contained a 33 lever Midland Railway tumbler frame and was commissioned on the 12th March 1905, replacing the North and South signal boxes. It closed on the 27th July 1980. It had been hoped to remove and preserve the box elsewhere but the poor condition of the timber framework put paid to the idea. Within a year of this photograph the glass in the station awnings would be condemned and removed. ***Graham Whitehead***

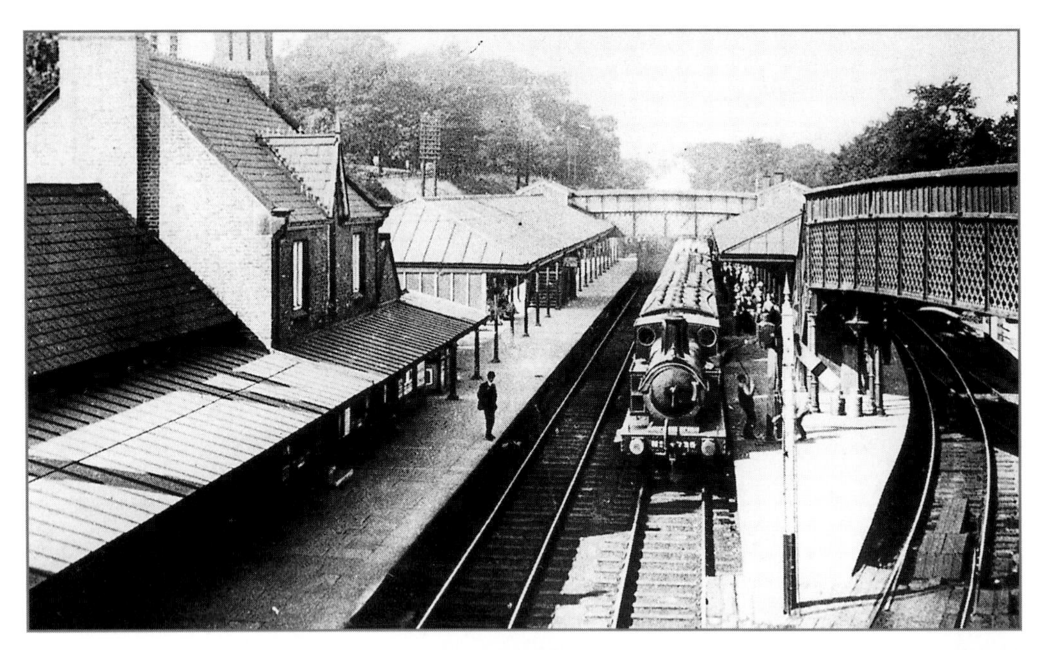

(Left) A view of Marple Station circa 1910. The station buildings remained substantially the same until demolition in the 1960s. The footbridge (No 26A) to the right provided a crucial link with Brabyns Brow in order to alleviate congestion during busy periods, on both this and the Down platform, which of course housed the main entrance and Booking Office. The signal partly obscures the locomotive crew operating the water crane, the bag of which is just being swung out of the locomotive's side tanks. This high summer scene shows a large group of people disembarking from the Great Central train. The fact that it has taken water suggests that it is going on to Hayfield. The locomotive is No **735**, a Class 3 2-4-2T, built at Gorton in 1892, to the design of Pollitt. ***courtesy W R Burton***

(Right) This view, looking down Brabyns Brow, around 1910, shows a line of open carriages awaiting the arrival of trains at Marple Station. These horse drawn vehicles were also used by day vistors who came to see the beauty spots in the area. The large sign to the right reads: *This way to Marple Bridge, Roman Bridge, Mellor and the Derbyshire hills,* pointing downhill. The hut belongs to the Bull's Head Livery Stables and the sign projecting from it announces that cabs may be called by telephone. ***Anon***

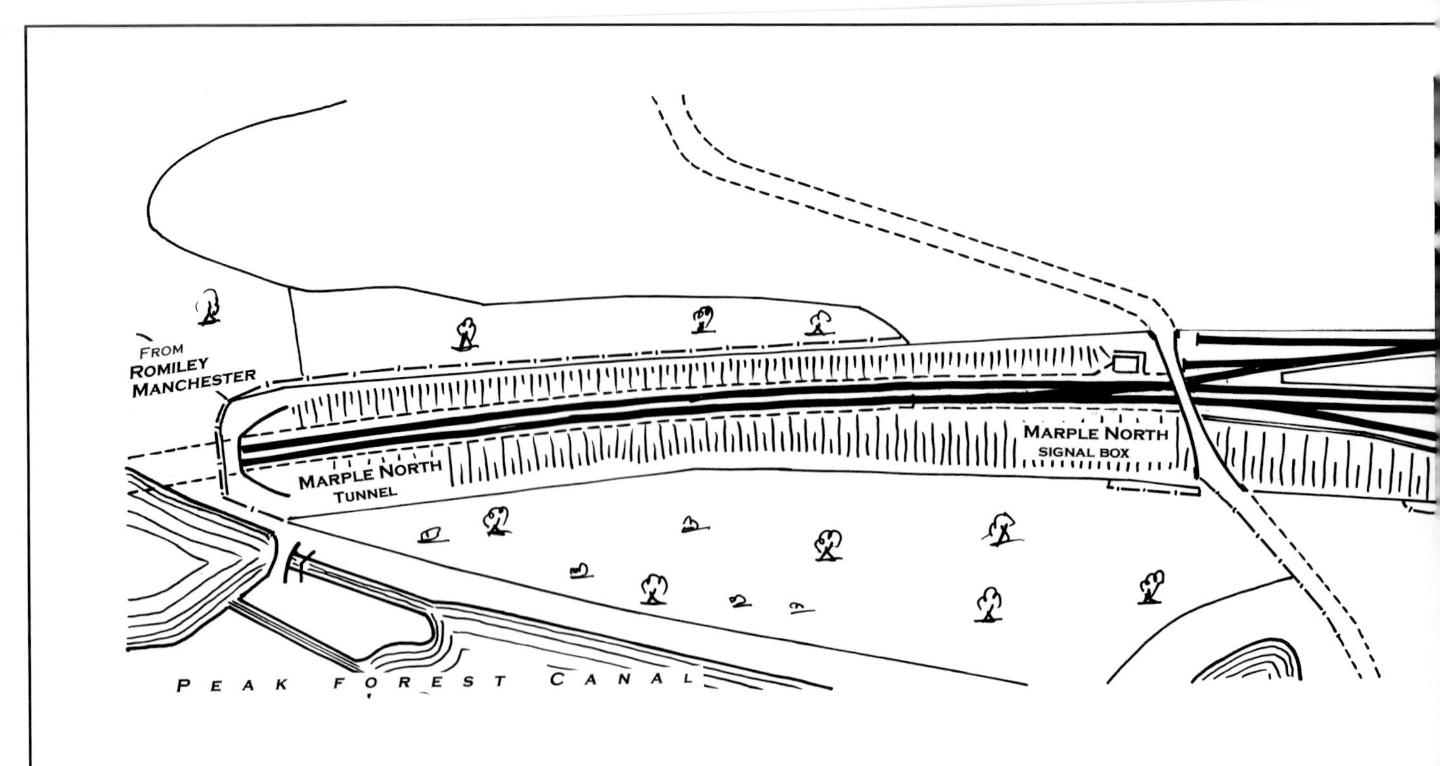

Continuing the period theme, this view from above the parapet walls of Brabyns Brow is thought to be around 1905. In the Down platform is a train of Great Central Railway six-wheeled carriages displaying the early livery of that company. In the Up Loop, an MS&L built Great Central liveried locomotive, possibly a Sacrê 4-4-0, seeks refuge with a passenger train. The footbridge which connects Brabyns Brow with the Up platform is thought to have been built about 1875. The Midland signal arm has a black roundel on white background, a feature which remained, generally, until about 1911. The ground, or dwarf, signal in the foreground was used to control movement of locomotives on and off the turntable which lay hard up against the retaining wall but was removed in 1914. It continued to be called the 'turntable road' until the curtailment of goods operations in 1964. On the extreme right, the end of a 10-ton wagon is shown in some detail, probably containing coal used at the station. ***Courtesy M A King***

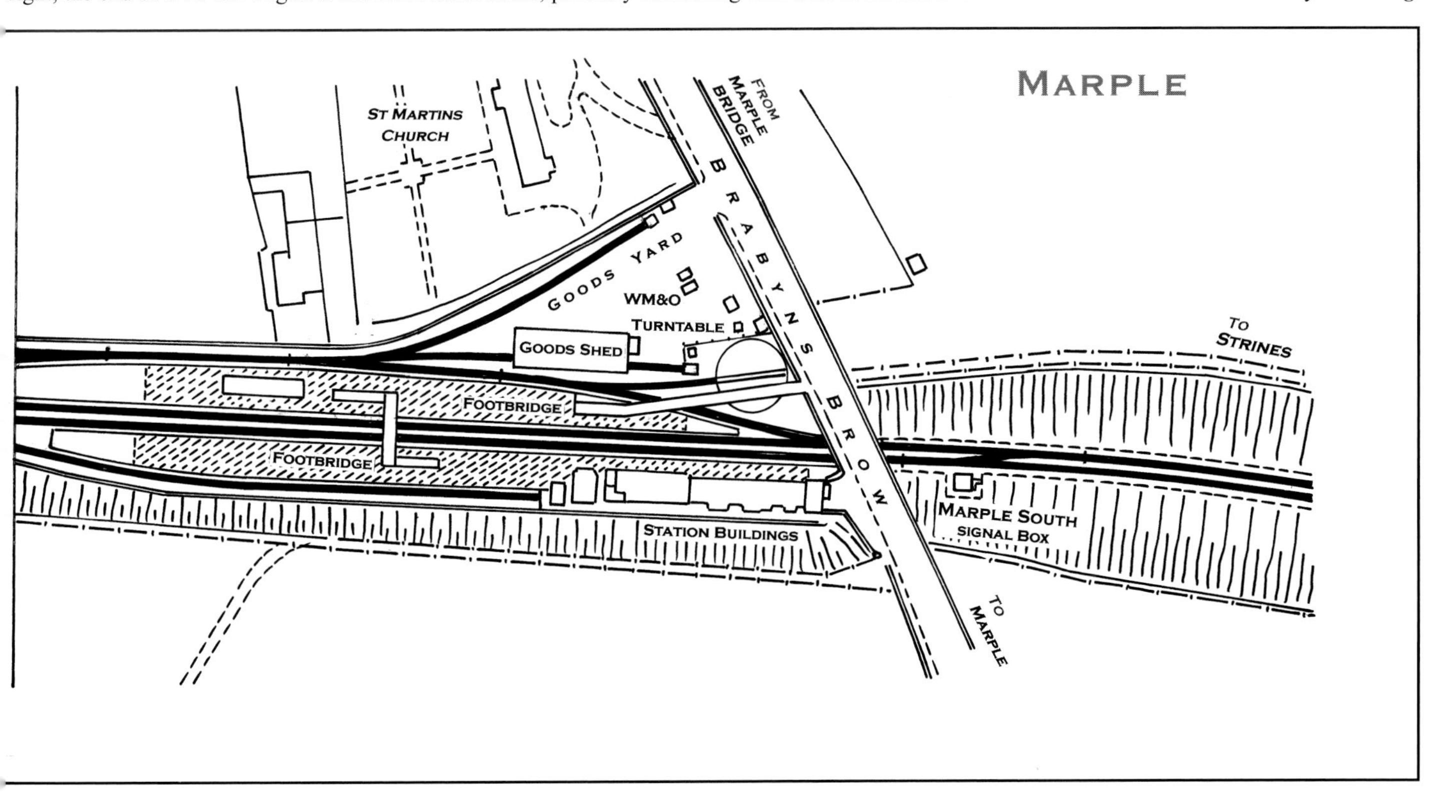

(Left) The main entrance to Marple Station was via the northbound (Down) platform. The entrance on Brabyns Brow is seen in this view of February 1964. The southbound (Up) platforms could also be reached by the long covered footbridge (No 26A), seen on the right of the picture, this somewhat unusual arrangement being caused by the presence of the Up Loop, Sidings, one time turntable, and the need to disperse passengers - commuters in particular - efficiently. The alternative was to cross the bridge further down the platform and face the prospect of another climb up several flights of stairs to the main entrance. ***Ian R Smith***

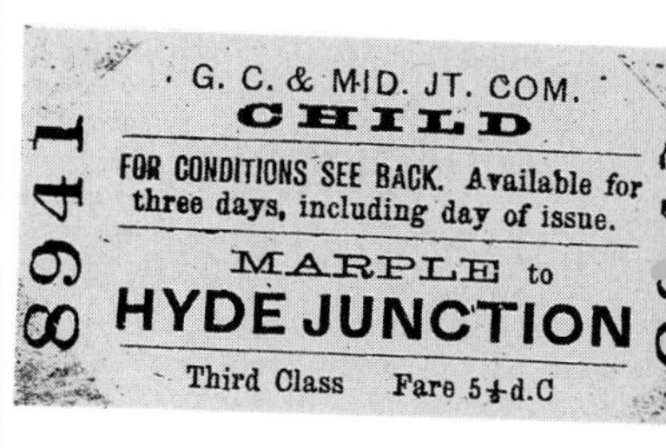

(Below-left) On a snowy morning in December 1964, crowds press forward as the 08.00 Hayfield – Manchester Piccadilly draws into Marple Station. This train ran non-stop from Marple to Manchester, taking 15 minutes for the journey. If there was a valuable legacy from one generation of rail travellers to another, then this working could be put forward as a prime candidate. The last public timetable produced by the Great Central Railway for 1922 detailed a train leaving Hayfield at 8.1am, due to call at Marple nineteen minutes later. Arrival in Manchester was timed for 8.42. An extract from *The Manchester Official ABC Railway Guide for February 1927* is reproduced at the bottom of the page showing an overall six minute improvement for the journey. The *Guide* cost 6d ($2^1/_2$p), the daily return fare from Marple being 2/3 d (11p), 3/9d First Class ! Between April 1966 and March 1967, the train was booked to leave Hayfield at 0800 and allowed 33 minutes for the journey to Piccadilly. The popularity of this train resulted in the crowds seen in this view. The six suburban non-corridor carriages with their high density seating would have required a ten car diesel multiple unit to cover this working. The train is hauled by an LMS built Fowler Class 4MT 2-6-4T. ***Ian R Smith***

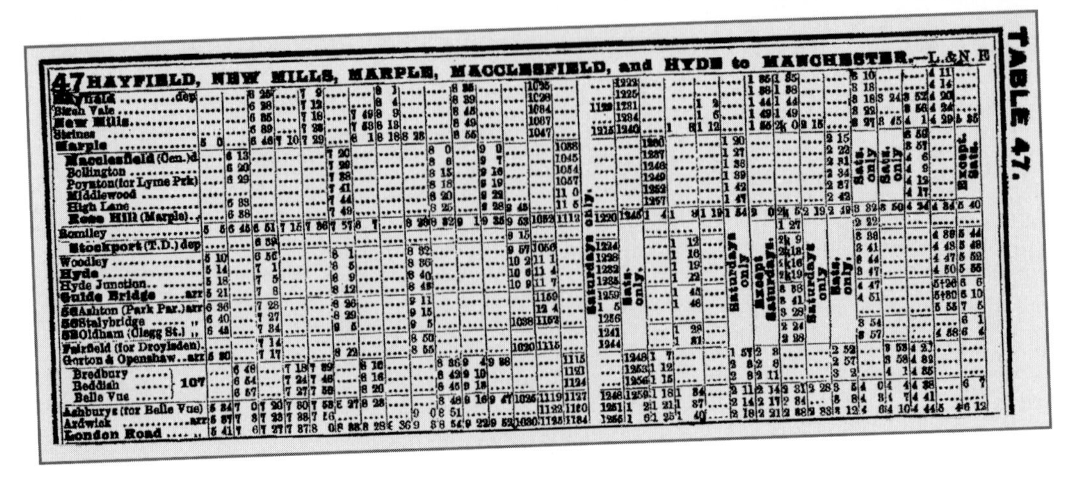

47 HAYFIELD, NEW MILLS, MARPLE, MACCLESFIELD, and HYDE to MANCHESTER.—L.&N.E. TABLE 47.

Hayfield ..... dep	[illegible]	[illegible]	[illegible]	[illegible]	[illegible]	[illegible]	[illegible]	[illegible]	[illegible]	[illegible]	[illegible]			1025			1222					1 35	1 35			3 10			4 11	
Birch Vale	[illegible]	[illegible]	[illegible]	[illegible]	[illegible]	[illegible]	[illegible]	[illegible]	[illegible]	[illegible]	[illegible]			1028			1225					1 38	1 38			3 13			4 14	
New Mills	[illegible]	[illegible]	[illegible]	[illegible]	[illegible]	[illegible]	[illegible]	[illegible]	[illegible]	[illegible]	[illegible]			1034		1129	1231			1 2		1 44	1 44			3 18	3 24	3 52	4 20	
Strines	[illegible]	[illegible]	[illegible]	[illegible]	[illegible]	[illegible]	[illegible]	[illegible]	[illegible]	[illegible]	[illegible]			1037			1234			1 6		1 49	1 49			3 22		3 56	4 24	
Marple	[illegible]	[illegible]	[illegible]	[illegible]	[illegible]	[illegible]	[illegible]	[illegible]	[illegible]	[illegible]	[illegible]			1047		1215	1240		1 8	1 12		1 55	2k0	2 15		3 27	3 45	4 1	4 29	5 35
Macclesfield (Cen.) dep	[illegible]	[illegible]	[illegible]	[illegible]	[illegible]	[illegible]	[illegible]	[illegible]	[illegible]	[illegible]	[illegible]	9 0			1038	Saturdays only.		1230			1 20				2 15	Sats. only	Sats. only	3 50		Except Sats.
Bollington	[illegible]	[illegible]	[illegible]	[illegible]	[illegible]	[illegible]	[illegible]	[illegible]	[illegible]	[illegible]	[illegible]	9 7			1045			1237			1 27				2 22			3 57		
Poynton (for Lyme Pk)	[illegible]	[illegible]	[illegible]	[illegible]	[illegible]	[illegible]	[illegible]	[illegible]	[illegible]	[illegible]	[illegible]	9 16			1054			1246			1 36				2 31			4 6		
Middlewood	[illegible]	[illegible]	[illegible]	[illegible]	7 41	[illegible]	[illegible]	8 20	[illegible]	[illegible]	[illegible]	9 19			1057			1249			1 39				2 34			4 9		
High Lane		6 33			7 44			8 25			9 28	9 22			11 0			1252			1 42				2 37			4 12		
Rose Hill (Marple)		6 38			7 49							9 28	9 45		11 5			1257			1 47				2 42			4 17		
Romiley	5 5	6 45	6 51	7 15	7 36	7 57	8 7		8 28	8 32	9 1	9 35	9 53	1052	1112	1220	1245	1 4	1 8	1 19	1 54	2 0	2k5	2 19	2 49	3 32	3 50	4 24	4 34	5 40
													9 15										1 27			3 22				
Stockport (T.D.) dep			6 39						8 32				9 57	1056		1224	Sats. only.		1 12		Saturdays only	Except Saturdays.	2k9	Saturdays only	Sats. only.	3 38			4 38	5 44
Woodley	5 10		6 56			8 1			8 36				10 2	11 1		1228			1 16				2k13			3 41			4 43	5 48
Hyde	5 14		7 1			8 5			8 40				10 6	11 4		1232			1 19				2k16			3 44			4 47	5 52
Hyde Junction	5 18		7 5			8 9			8 43				10 9	11 7		1235			1 22				2k19			3 47			4 50	5 55
Guide Bridge .... arr	5 21		7 8			8 12			8 46					1159		1259			1 45				3 38			4 47			5†26	6 6
56 Ashton (Park Par.) arr	6 36		7 28			8 26			9 11					12 4		1 5			1 48				3 41			4 51			5†30	6 10
56 Stalybridge .... „	6 40		7 27			8 29			9 15				1038	1152		1256							3 28						5 55	7 5
58 Oldham (Clegg St.) „	6 48		7 34			9 5			9 5							1241			1 28				2 24			3 54				6 1
Fairfield (for Droylsden)			7 14						8 50				1020	1115		1244			1 31				2 28			3 57			4 58	6 4
Gorton & Openshaw .. arr	5 30		7 17			8 22			8 55																					
Bredbury ..... (107)		6 48		7 18	7 39		8 10			8 36	9 4	9 36			1115		1248	1 7			1 57	2 8			2 52		3 53	4 2		
Reddish ..... (107)		6 54		7 24	7 46		8 16			8 42	9 10				1120		1253	1 12			2 3	2 8			2 57		3 58	4 32		
Belle Vue ..... (107)		6 57		7 27	7 50		8 20			8 45	9 13				1124		1256	1 15			2 8	2 11			3 2		4 1	4 35		
Ashburys (for Belle Vue)	5 34	7 0	7 20	7 30	7 53	8 27	8 28			8 48	9 16	9 47	1026	1119	1127	1248	1259	1 18		1 34	2 11	2 14	2 31	2 28	3 5	4 0	4 4	4 38		6 7
Ardwick .... arr	5 37	7 3	7 23	7 33	[illegible]	[illegible]	[illegible]			8 51	[illegible]	[illegible]	[illegible]	1122	1120	1251	1 2	1 21		1 37	2 14	2 17	2 34	[illegible]	3 8	4 3	4 7	4 41	4 44	6 12
London Road ..... „	5 41	7 6	[illegible]	[illegible]	[illegible]	[illegible]	[illegible]	[illegible]	[illegible]	[illegible]	[illegible]	[illegible]	[illegible]	[illegible]	[illegible]	[illegible]	[illegible]	[illegible]	[illegible]	[illegible]	[illegible]	[illegible]	[illegible]	[illegible]	[illegible]	[illegible]	[illegible]	[illegible]	[illegible]	[illegible]

(Above) One of the impressive Class L1 2-6-4Ts, No **67751 (**Built 1948 - North British Loco. Co) is about to depart from Marple with the 17.29 Manchester London Road – Hayfield train on 20th September 1958. The use of steam on Hayfield trains by this time was restricted to rush hour workings. The same restriction applied to ex-GCR A5 Class 4-6-2T No **69801**, seen in the Up Loop platform. Normally locomotives faced south so the bunker-first appearance of 69801 is unusual. The rolling stock on the Hayfield train was formed of non-corridor suburban carriages, the first being a BR Mark 1 with the rest being of LNER Thompson design. ***R Keeley***

(Left-centre) The view looking south from the Up Loop at Marple. The short siding, used by coal merchants, originally gave access to a 50ft turntable which was taken out of use in 1914. However, owing to restricted space in the goods yards and difficult access on to the fearsome Brabyns Brow, most local coal merchants favoured the facilities at Rose Hill Station a mile away on the Macclesfield line. This view, taken on 30th March 1960 shows a Midland lower quadrant signal almost underneath the long overbridge providing the exit for passengers from southbound trains. One of the authors (*IRS*) tried to buy this signal when the loop was lifted but was advised by BR that it was not for sale! ***J A Peden Collection***

Marple Goods Yard was a difficult site to operate. It involved trains using the east loop and pushing wagons as far as seen in this photograph. Owing to weight restrictions, locomotives were not allowed to go any further on the outside line and wagons had to be manoeuvred by using extra wagons to give length. In this view, dated 30th March 1960, Class J11 0-6-0 No **64341** has pushed an engineers' wagon on to the outside line. The operation is overseen by the Station Master whilst the Shunter (with pole) watches the wagons further along. The middle line led to the goods shed. Marple lost its goods facilities when they were withdrawn on 5th October 1964. ***J A Peden Collection***

Marple Station looking north on 21st April 1935, sees LMS Class 4 Compound 4-4-0 No **1089** about to leave with a train for Chinley. Judging by the rolling stock, this was probably one of the Manchester Victoria – Chinley expresses which provided connections for passengers from north of Manchester into southbound expresses at Chinley. These trains were stopped with the advent of the Second World War and never resumed afterwards. ***J A Peden Collection***

(Left) A 1968 view of Marple Station after the removal of the glazing from the platform awnings, and the roof from the footbridge. These alterations were harbingers of the dereliction to come. On the right the Up Loop line has been lifted and the platform edge fenced off. The signal post restricted height upper quadrant starter signal looks recently painted and was to survive for a further decade. The train in the northbound platform is a later style of Derby 'lightweight' diesel multiple unit. Forming an afternoon Marple – Manchester Piccadilly service, it has crossed over from the Up to the Down side by using the crossover located beneath the road overbridge (Brabyns Brow) from which the photograph was taken. ***BR(LMR)***

Marple Station on 31st March 1966 during the period when it was being shorn of much of its surplus operational facilities. The Up Loop and Down bay have been lifted, as has the goods yard to the left of the signalbox. A brand new English Electric Type 1 (Class 20) diesel locomotive is heading south through Marple en route from its birthplace at Vulcan Foundry (Earlestown) to Doncaster where it would be inspected before official acceptance into traffic. Although its number is not recorded it would have been in the batch D8132-35 which were introduced that month. ***Ian R Smith***

(Right-centre) Marple Station north end on 11th April 1966 sees BR/Sulzer Type 2 No **D5225** (Class 25, later 25 075) heading the 14.05 (SO) Blackpool North – Nottingham Midland. On the left the connection from the Down bay has been removed whilst a dismantled gangers' trolley, used in the demolition of Marple Station and its associated trackwork, is on the platform opposite. ***Ian R Smith***

(Below) Trafford Park (9E) based Class 5MT 4-6-0 No **45269** brings a Manchester Central – Sheffield train into Marple Station on 24th July 1964. The signal box, dating from 1905, was certainly custom made - almost non-standard - for its location, given the restrictions on viewing by the platform canopy. Already the bay platform (left) and Up Loop platform (behind the signal box) had been removed. The water cranes still survive at the ends of the platforms, as did the glazing in the station canopies, albeit still painted black as a wartime air raid prevention measure. ***A Moyes***

(Right) Marple Station in December 1964, following the removal of the goods shed and associated trackwork. The footbridge from the island platform to Brabyns Brow was destined to survive another five years owing to budgetary indecisions. ***Ian R Smith***

MARPLE RENAISSANCE

(Right-centre) In March 1970 the long footbridge (26A) linking the southbound platform with Brabyns Brow was demolished. In this view a crane is lifting out one of the displaced sections. Originally an open structure, as seen in this view, it was later roofed, panelled in wood and glazed. The roof was re-covered in 1946. In the background the former goods yard was already being used as a car park by rail users. ***North Cheshire Herald***

(Below-left) View looking north at Marple Station on 20th April 1970 showing the southbound platform cleared of all buildings apart from the signal box. The footbridge remained, shorn of its wooden panelling, glazing and roof. The new station offices are under construction on the southbound platform whilst those they will replace are still providing some limited cover on the northbound platform. ***Ian R Smith***

(Below-right) Marple Station was officially reopened on 28th October 1970. In this view, Councillor M T Burton, Chairman of Marple Urban District Council (and also a railwayman) signals away the first train to leave after the opening ceremony. This was the 12.33 Marple – Manchester formed of a Birmingham R C & W Co (later Class 104) diesel multiple unit. ***North Cheshire Herald***

Pulling away from Marple Station, Class 5MT 4-6-0 No **44815** (9E) heads the 13.45 Manchester Central – Sheffield Midland train on 13th April 1966 beneath Brabyns Brow. This was quite a stern test for a heavily loaded train as the immediate effect of the 1 in 100 gradient would be apparent. This train also provided a connection at Chinley for Hope Valley and Sheffield bound passengers off the 14.00 Manchester Central to Nottingham Midland service which had travelled over the direct line via Cheadle Heath. The area to the right is the site of a 50ft turntable, installed in 1898. To the left was the location of Marple South signal box that was replaced in 1905 by the commissioning of Marple Station box on the Up platform. ***Ian R Smith***

The northbound or Down platform at Marple Station always dealt with more originating business than that on the opposite side. This view shows the station in 1968, just before the platform awnings were removed. The tall building on the left housed the elegant stairway from Brabyns Brow. The single storey buildings contained the booking and parcels offices whilst the house was the residence of successive Station Masters. This combination of structures had similarities with those at New Mills and Hayfield although the latter did not have the small central gable in the roof. The small extension to its right was the Porters' room. The wooden framed building on the extreme right was an elegant General Waiting Room with bay windows from which trains could be watched whilst basking in the warmth of a roaring coal fire on cold days. ***BR(LMR)***

The view from Brabyns Brow looking south. On 15th February 1969, English Electric Type 4 No **291** (later Class 40 091) approaches Marple Station. The point controlling the crossover used by multiple units turning back at Marple is seen at the bottom of the view. The benefits of electrically-heated points are evident in the severe weather conditions which had deposited several inches of snow in the area overnight. Note the 45mph speeed restriction sign which applied to the curves either side of Marple South tunnel. ***Ian R Smith***

(Above) Climbing to Marple South Tunnel with the empty stock of a Leeds – Belle Vue excursion, Class 5MT No **44897** heads for Gowhole on 30th April 1967.

(Above-right) The line south from Marple Statio is cut into the hillside, creating a stee embankment on the Down (west) side, whist o the Up (east) side the land falls steeply awa behind the trees to the River Goyt. Climbin towards Marple South Tunnel English Electri Type 4 No **D246** (Class 40, later 40 046) headin the empty stock of a Castleford – Belle Vu excursion on 30th May 1967. The train is about t enter Marple South Tunnel.

(Left) The northern portal of Marple South Tunn is seen as English Electric Type 4 No **D291** (Clas 40, later 40 091) drifts downgrade with a train c limestone hopper wagons belonging to ICI. The cas iron name sign declares that the tunnel is 225 yard (206 metres) long, although the Midland Railwa register gives it as 224 yards. Also according to th register, the tunnel was shortened at the north end b some 45 yards in 1874/75. It is also difficult t appreciate that in 1933, the LMS had found necessary to modify the tunnel to allow gaug clearance for Third Class 68ft sleeper carriages

All (3); ***Ian R Smi***

(Right) Marple South Tunnel, New Mills end, looking north, circa 1955. The close proximity of Lakes Road, which crosses the railway just north of the tunnel entrance, gave the constructors of the line an added problem. With the adjacent land falling away rapidly and the road running virtually parallel, the option to have a longer tunnel with very little cover was rejected in favour of the substantial retaining wall that is seen here to the right. Once again the very restricted nature of the 'cess' and acute batter of the masonry resulted in the calibration of the line being indicated by a mile 'plate' rather than the usual triangular shaped casting mounted on a section of old rail. The distance was 176¼ miles from St Pancras and the plate is to the extreme right of the picture. ***D Ibbotson***

(Right-centre) Bursting out of Marple South Tunnel on 12th April 1966, Class 5MT 4-6-0 No **45096** (Agecroft - 9J) raises the echoes whilst working uphill with the empty stock of a West Riding – Belle Vue excursion on its way to New Mills South. The difficulties of building and maintaining this section of line are evident in this view. ***Ian R Smith***

(Below- left) The cramped confines of the southern opening of Marple South Tunnel are evident in this view. Brush A1A-A1A Type 2 No **D5844** (Class 31, later 31 310) of Sheffield Darnall, makes light work of the three coach 11.45 Manchester Central – Sheffield Midland train on 12th April 1966. By this time the locomotive diagrams worked by Sheffield crews had gone over to diesel haulage whilst those operated by Trafford Park (Manchester) crews were still steam-hauled. ***Ian R Smith***

(Below-right) Drifting downhill from Strines, a train of 'empties' from Gowhole to Dewsnap is headed by Class 5MT 4-6-0 No **45382** (Newton Heath - 9D). The train is about to enter Marple South Tunnel on 12th April 1966 ***Ian R Smith***

(Above-left) An engineers' train descends towards the entrance of Marple South Tunnel behind BR/Sulzer Type 2 (Class 24) No **D5053** (24 053) on 19th April 1968. Looking south, it is noticable that the railway is constructed on a shelf hewn out of the steep-sided Goyt Valley, which opens out in earnest on the left hand side as the line climbs towards Strines.

(Above) A six-car formation of Derby Lightweight DMUs (later Class 108) heads wrong line - owing to engineering work on Goyt Cliff Viaduct - away from Marple South Tunnel with the Sundays Only 10.32 Manchester Central - Sheffield Midland on 10th December 1967. This was a working that began at Liverpool Lime Street (Depart 09.30), providing an opportunity for hikers from Merseyside and the Manchester area to gain access to the Hope Valley stations.

Derby Lightweight diesel multiple unit accelerates towards Arkwright's Bridge with the 11.00 Manchester Piccadilly – Hayfield train on 17th August 1965. Note to the left the 45mph speed restriction sign which was in force on the curves approaching Marple South Tunnel. Although the line speed between New Mills and Romiley was 60mph, there had since the 1890s been a limit at this location following a serious landslip on Sunday, December 24th 1893, which closed the line for two days. The retaining wall constructed as a result of this mishap is just visible at the rear of the train to the right. A clearer view of the site can be seen in the picture above (right).

The adverse gradients on the climb to New Mills will not unduly tax the crew of this lightweight southbound goods train as it approaches Arkwright's Bridge, the point at which the line levelled out on the approach to Goyt Viaduct. Class 8F 2-8-0 No **48612** is hauling empty coal wagons on a train from north Manchester to Gowhole on 17th August 1965. The locomotive was based at Newton Heath. All: ***Ian R Smith***

(Above) This view of an unidentified 'Jubilee' crossing Marple's Goyt Cliff viaduct on 20th June 1961(Tuesday) highlights the lush beauty of the Goyt Valley. The Jubilees were by now well down the pecking order in terms of main line duty but locally they enjoyed something of a celebrity status, particularly at the head of the afternoon Liverpool - Nottingham 'express'. On this occasion however, we have the 4.5pm Manchester Central to Sheffield Midland (arr. 6.6pm) train, booked to call at all stations via Stockport Tiviot Dale and the Hope Valley. On Saturdays, an extra four minutes was allowed for the journey. Four of the five masonry openings at the south end of the viaduct are in view here. The river passes beneath the metal span located beneath the third carriage of the train. ***John Oldham***

(Right) Class 5 4-6-0 No **45071** (Speke Junction - 8C) heads the 15.30 Manchester Central – Sheffield Midland across Goyt Cliff Viaduct in August 1965. Unusually the train was composed of four BR Mark 1 non-corridor suburban carriages. ***Ian R Smith***

Some 161 yards in length, Goyt Cliff Viaduct (No 23), as identified by the Midland Railway Company, spanned both land and the River Goyt. There were five masonry spans over land at the south end, each of 45 feet with a 2ft 9in thick arch ring. A further two arches were over land at the northern end, these having the same dimensions as the other five. The main span however, giving eight in total, was constructed using wrought iron, and was 82 feet in length. Main, deck and cross girders, together with lattice parapets, were all of the same material. An 1893 strengthening programme resulted in a centre girder of steel being added. It is interesting to note that in a structural report (circa 1880) by engineers of the *Sheffield & Midland Committee,* the structure is referred to as 'Windybottom Viaduct'.

(Right-upper) Crossing Goyt Cliff Viaduct, a Derby Lightweight (Class 108) diesel multiple unit four-car set works the 15.00 Manchester Piccadilly to Hayfield on 15th July 1967. The front car is in the BR overall blue livery whilst the rear three are still wearing the obsolete lined green livery. The viaduct has a substantial metal span over the Goyt waterfall and this was one of the reasons for the delay in construction of the Marple – New Mills section of line. Through the left hand arch of the viaduct can be seen the car park of the Roman Lakes.

Ian R Smith

(Right-centre) The dominating presence of the structure is evident in this view from the west side. Of necessity, the railway required a substantial structure to bridge the Goyt waterfall to the left of this 1906 picture. Webb's Tea Rooms were part of a popular tourist trap in the days before cars. With the nearby 'Roman' Bridge and Lakes, many day trippers would come to Marple and either walk to these delightful spots or use horse-drawn transport available at Marple Station.

A Hulme

A BR/Sulzer Type 2 rushes an afternoon Sheffield – Manchester Central train across the viaduct on 28th December 1966. The LMS built coaching stock was nearing the end of its life as, indeed was the service to Manchester Central.

Ian R Smith

(Right) Accelerating off Goyt Cliff Viaduct and facing the half a mile at 1 in 100 to Strines, a southbound Blackpool – Sheffield Midland train is headed by BR/Sulzer Type 2 (Class 25) Nos **D7583** (25 233) and **D5235** (25 085) on 15th July 1967. This Saturdays Only train ran during the summer months only and travelled via Manchester Victoria and Ashburys. It is becoming noticeable that lineside vegetation is encroaching as maintenance methods change, local gangs being gradually phased out in favour of a supposedly more mobile operation from fewer depots. No more controlled lineside fires, even the 'art' of ballast edging seems already to have disappeared. It is also perhaps worth noting that although both locos were still less than five years old, neither lasted more than nineteen years in service.

Ian R Smith

(Centre) 'Jubilee' Class 6P5F 4-6-0 No **45581** *Bihar and Orissa* (Farnley Junction - 55C) makes light work of the climb from Goyt Cliff Viaduct to Strines with the empty stock of a Leeds – Belle Vue excursion on 31st May 1966. The line, having swept around a 120 chain radius over the viaduct, straightens out for a short distance prior to reverse curves that will end at Strines. The train was taken to New Mills South Goods Yard to be stabled whilst the locomotive went to Heaton Mersey for servicing. ***Ian R Smith***

(Right) Ascending the stretch of line (19th June 1965) which enjoys splendid views across the Goyt Valley, this 2-car 'original' Derby Lightweight DMU will have made light work of this evening train, the 19.00 Manchester Piccadilly to Hayfield via Reddish, indeed the most arduous section was still to come after leaving New Mills with almost two miles of climbing before it, initially at 1 in 78 before easing off at 1 in 99. The $15^{1}/_{2}$ mile journey was booked to take 44 minutes. Unit No 79173, a Motor Brake Second, was built at Derby Works in May 1956 to work as a twin with other similar units. It is hard to believe that British Railways had a return of only eleven years use out of the vehicle before its withdrawal in 1967. ***M Mensing***

(Above) The embankment that carried the line between Marple and Strines is shown to good effect in this view across the valley from the Peak Forest canal near Strines. The train is a railtour organised by the nascent Severn Valley Railway on 20th April 1968 and hauled by Class 5MT 4-6-0s Nos **44781** and **45046.** This section of the tour ran from Stockport Edgeley to Buxton, then to Stalybridge where the locomotives gave way to two BR Standard Class 5MT 4-6-0s. ***J R Hillier***

(Centre) Running northbound down the 1 in 100 gradient from Strines, English Electric Type 4 No **D390** (Class 40 190) passes Strawberry Hill on 12th June 1968. The outer signals operated by Strines signal box can be seen in the distance. The chimney belongs to the Strines Print Works. The large number of telegraph wires indicates how busy the line had been in the past before the advances brought about by fibre optic cabling and the like.
Ian R Smith

(Right-lower) BR 7P6F 'Britannia' Class Pacifics were used on Midland line expresses between Manchester Central and London St Pancras from 1956 until 1960 during electrification of the Euston to Liverpool and Manchester routes. The use of one of the class, No **70002** *Geoffrey Chaucer* (Carlisle-Kingmoor - 12A), in August 1965 was most unusual. Seen here accelerating downhill from Strines to Marple, all was not as it might seem for this was the empty stock working for a return Belle Vue – West Riding excursion.
Ian R Smith

Strines station was perched high on the hillside, a good distance from the community it served and largely hidden from view by a shallow cutting within the landscape. The small goods yard was well suited to serve the nearby Strines Print (textiles) Works although much of the business from that source was directed via the freight arrangements in nearby New Mills. Public freight facilities were withdrawn from 12th August 1963 and the station was de-staffed from 10th September 1973.

(Above-right) English Electric Type 4 No **D222** *Laconia* (Class 40 022) heads a loaded limestone train through Strines on 10th July 1968. The train originated in the Buxton area and, judging by the four wheeled hopper wagons, would probably be destined for BR track renewal in the Manchester area. ***Ian R Smith***

(Centre) An undated summertime view of a Derby lightweight diesel multiple unit four car set leaving Strines on a Hayfield – Manchester Piccadilly working. ***Ian R Smith***

(Below) On 17th May 1963, B1 Class 4-6-0 No **61093** (Canklow - 41D) leaves Strines with an afternoon Sheffield Midland – Manchester Central train. The rural and isolated setting of Strines station is particularly striking in this view. Its main purpose was to service the print works in the valley. ***A Moyes***

(Right) Showing an incorrect *Chinley* destination, an Eastern Region Derby Lightweight diesel multiple unit (later Class 114) leaves Strines on a snowy 11th December 1967. Following withdrawal of local train services from Manchester Central, these trains were diverted to Piccadilly, running non-stop between Romiley and Manchester. The Up (southbound) waiting shelter can just be seen behind the signal post. The signal box, with a 12-lever tumbler frame, was commisioned by theMidland Railway in 1893, replacing an earlier structure, can be seen beyond the footbridge. The main station facilities were housed in the attractive stone building behind the train. ***Ian R Smith***

Strines Station on 29th March 1967. 8F Class 2-8-0 8F No **48376** (Buxton - 9L) labours up the incline from Marple with a ballast train. The view, taken from the footbridge shows the station master's house and ticket office on the Down (northbound) platform. Illumination was provided by gas; the fittings for which were modernised in 1960. Passing freight trains were a frequent occurrence whereas the yard at Strines, according to *WTT for 15th September 1952,* had just one, Target 92, arriving from New Mills Goods at 11.5am, and being allowed twenty five minutes to carry out shunting duties before departing for New Mills again. Engine and crew for the trip originated at Gowhole. ***Ian R Smith***

(Right) A view looking north along a deserted Down platform from under the footbridge at Strines on 9th August 1969. Constructed in the traditional way for the time, the footbridge comprised main girders of Wrought Iron supported on Cast Iron columns. It was numbered 17A by the Midland Railway, the 'A' suffix being added because the structure was not erected until 1884. It was considered surplus to requirements when the station became unstaffed and subsequently removed. The attractive waiting shelter of Midland origin, together with the station buildings, were replaced by simple stone shelters. ***Stations UK***

(Above) Strines, c.1956. We will forever be indebted to photographer W A (Allan) Brown for recording not only this but many of the 1950s views seen elsewhere within the pages of this book. Minor accessories apart, such as updated signalling, coaching stock and liveries, this scene mirrored the 'Hayfield' line as it had been for the best part of half a century. Although into its fourth decade of service, C14 4-4-2T No **67448** - built by Beyer Peacock in 1924 - was representing a basic design that had first seen light of day in 1903 under Great Central stewardship. The loco is seen here pulling away from Strines with a Manchester bound train. ***W A Brown***

(Below-right) Strines Station in the 1950s. The booking clerk has crossed from the Up (southbound) to the Down (northbound) platform, choosing to cross the lines rather than use the nearby footbridge. Platforms on most stations with minimal staffing however had 'strategically' placed projections from the platform wall for staff to avail themselves of the shortest route back to the booking office. The main buildings contained similar features to be found at both Hayfield and New Mills although on a smaller scale. Beyond the footbridge is the wooden goods shed, similar in style to those at Marple, Hayfield and Woodley. Behind that were two short goods sidings with a capacity for 32 wagons. ***Mowat Collection***

Strines, c.1956. The footbridge at Strines was always a popular vantage point for photographers. During the summer months, the variety and volume of traffic passing through could be quite substantial. The steady climb from Marple supplied the added ingredient of syncopation from the varied motive power that was thrust into action, in particular the numerous Belle Vue excursion trains that somehow had to be dispersed. Back to the view here however and it is the humble local train that is the centre of attraction as a Class A5 eases alongside the platform with a Hayfield bound train. Loco apart, the scene is ostensively Midland, with lamp standards, fencing, running in (nameboard), all of Derby origin. The shelter to the right, although from a drawing produced by the Midland Railway architects at Derby, also had certain features found in buildings produced by the lines' joint promoters, the MS&L. ***W A Brown***

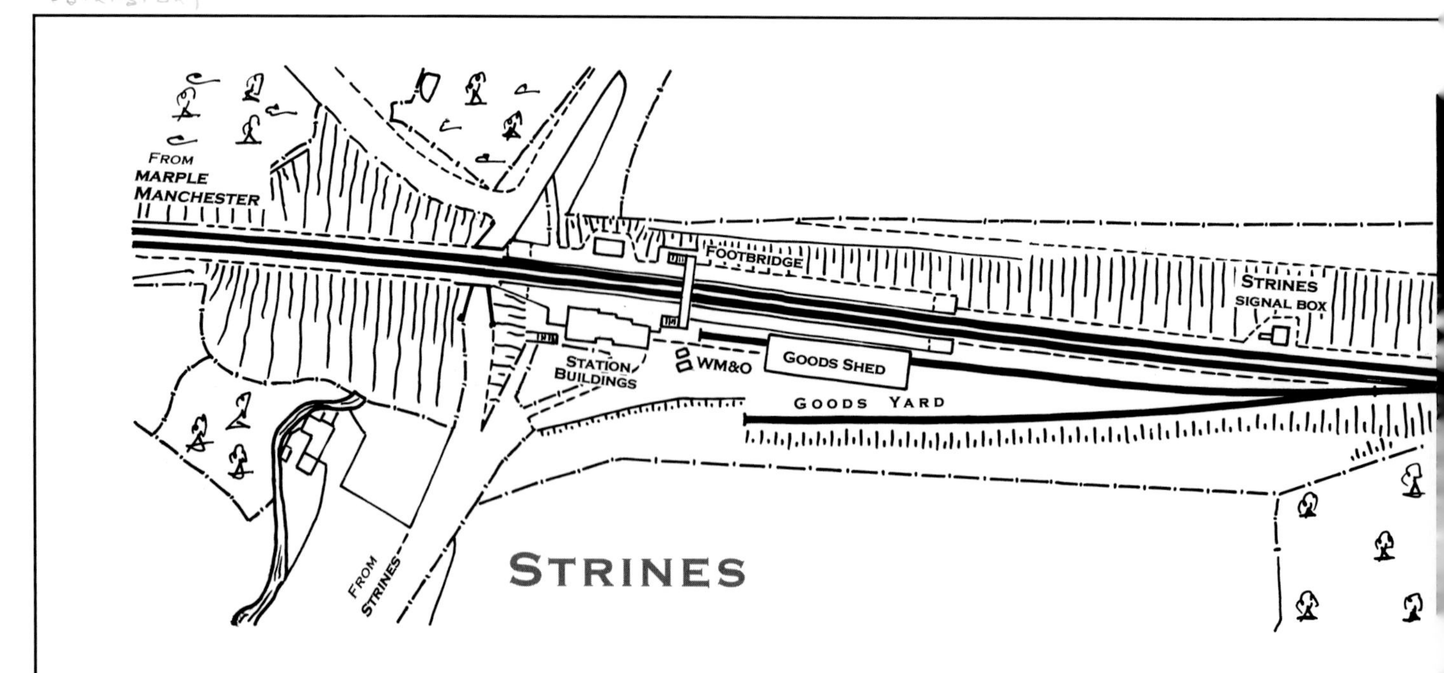

Canklow based B1 Class 4-6-0 No **61370** restarts the 15.30 Manchester Central – Sheffield Midland at Strines on 26th April 1963. This North British built loco was to a 1942 design by LNER Chief Mechanical Engineer Edward Thompson, successor to Sir Nigel Gresley, and left the works new in 1950. The goods shed and yard show little if any sign of activity. Although closure was not very far away, the final curtain on freight operation was in the August of 1963. The remaining wagon load traffic was transferred to New Mills Goods and the track and buildings subsequently dismantled.The journey from Manchester to Sheffield via Stockport Tiviot Dale and the Hope Valley was certainly one to savour and the all stations nature of the trip took full advantage of the nominal two hours allowed. ***A Moyes***

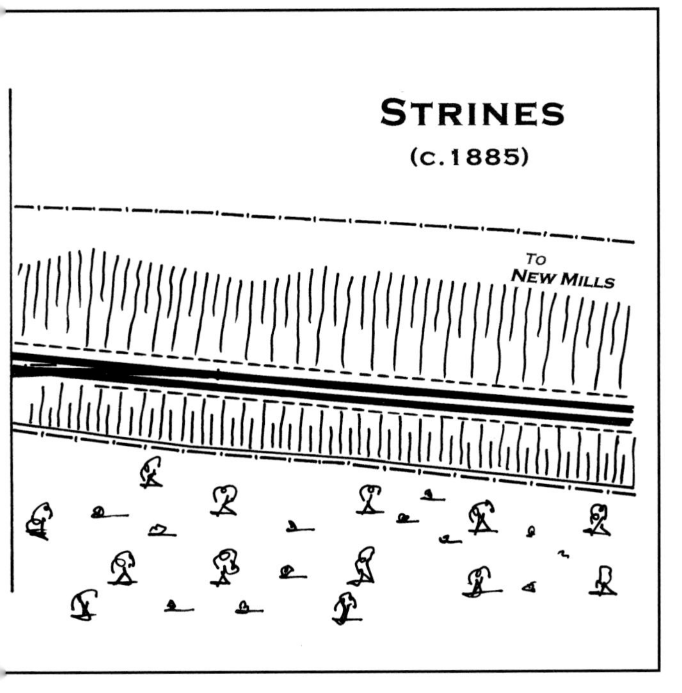

A view of Strines Station Down (northbound) platform from a diverted Manchester Central – London St Pancras express in 1959. Note the platform seating arrangements at a time when four and five coach trains were the norm. Only basic passenger facilities now remain. ***Anon***

(Above) A view of Strines Station, looking in the direction of New Mills in 1898. The footbridge (1884) was a standard design of the Midland Railway for the period and would give another seven decades of use before its removal in 1972. The station master and another member of the station staff are posed for the photograph. ***Anon***

(Right-centre) Strines Station on 16th April 1966. A rail tour organised by the Locomotive Club of Great Britain races along with a four coach train of LMS - built corridor coaches, hauled by BR Standard Class 3 2-6-2T No **82003**. This was probably the only time a locomotive of this class ever visited the line as none was ever allocated to the area until this one reached Patricroft (Manchester) in 1966. A few months later it was withdrawn from service. This tour of various threatened lines in the Manchester area visited Hayfield. Whilst most of the gas lamps had been renewed by 1960, the one on the right of the picture, positioned above the landing of the footbridge to illuminate the steps, still sported its Midland top. ***Ian R Smith***

(Right-lower) Seen from the former goods yard, now devoid of rails and other fittings, BR/Sulzer 1Co-Co1 Type 4 No **D47** (later Class 45 116) arrives with the 13.45 Manchester Central – Sheffield Midland train on 28th December 1966, just days before the service ceased. ***Ian R Smith***

(Right) By the summer of 1965 the goods sidings at Strines had been taken out and the former connection clipped and padlocked. A van belonging to the signalman was parked at the throat of the erstwhile yard. Facing the gradient towards New Mills, British Railways built B1 Class 4-6-0 No **61384** is about to restart the 13.45 Manchester Central – Sheffield Midland.
Ian R Smith

(Centre) Strines, 27th April 1968. It was still possible during the final months of steam operation on British Railways to see loose coupled freight trains moving slowly about the system in time honoured tradition. The scene we have here is no exception as Newton Heath (9D) 8F 2-8-0 No **48373** heads a short train of mineral wagons through Strines some ten minutes after leaving Gowhole Sidings. The likely destination is Brewery Sidings (Miles Platting), a journey time of about one hour, approximately fifteen miles away.
J W Sutherland

(Below) Strines, c.1953. A Manchester London Road – Hayfield train climbs away from Strines and towards the cutting at Hague Bar. The entrance to Strines goods yard is to the right of the picture. The train, probably hauled by one of the Great Central 4-4-2T locomotives then currently on the line, comprises two former Great Central coaches, an LNER built Gresley coach and two BR Mark 1 suburban coaches. All stock used on Hayfield trains was invariably non-corridor. The schoolboys waving from the train is a reminder of the days when the line was responsible for significant numbers of 'Contract' holders; these were children who were given season tickets by their local education authorities for travel to secondary schools.
Eric Oldham

(Above) Strines, 19th February 1949. Still in LNER livery, Class C13 (GCR Class 9K - built 1904) 4-4-2T No **7423** leaves Strines (depart 3.12pm) with the 2.23pm Manchester London Road to Hayfield via Hyde train. This being a Saturday, it was due to pass the 3.00pm (SO) Hayfield to London Road - also via Hyde - working at Strines. It is possible to see the rear of that train in the distance as it passes the signal box just south of the station. Although still a winter's day with little in the way of foliage to announce the coming of spring, the surroundings formed just one of numerous parts of the Goyt Valley that were easily accessible by rail. Between the wars, the area was particularly attractive to groups from Manchester. Special trains were frequently arranged to bring the parties for a day out in the countryside. One such event in May 1929 was arranged for Wesleyan Chapels and Sunday Schools in the Broughton Park, Crumpsall, Cheetham Hill and Miles Platting districts of Manchester. With advertised stops at Romiley (Broughton Park Cong. S.S and Cheetham Hill Wesleyans - *50 Adults, 120 Children*), Strines (Lower Crumpsall Wesleyans - *120 Adults, 80 Children*) and Birch Vale (St. Luke's S.S, Miles Platting - *100 Adults, 150 Children*) upwards of some 600 individuals would be transported. After calling at Birch Vale, the train would run empty to Hayfield where the carriages would be stabled for the day. The locomotive would then work light engine to Belle Vue for servicing and spend the day on shed before returning to Hayfield for an early evening departure with the inward bound train.
J D Darby

(Right-centre) Pulling away from Strines, Class 5MT 4-6-0 No **44888** (Trafford Park - 9E) enters the cutting at Hague Bar with the 15.30 Manchester Central – Sheffield Midland train during the summer of 1966. The train comprises four BR Mark 1 corridor coaches.
Ian R Smith

(Right-lower) With lengthening evening shadows, Class 4P (3-Cyl. Compound) 4-4-0 No **41048** (Bedford - 15D) climbs away from Strines and bites in as it attacks the incline through the cutting at Hague Bar. This 1953 view shows a Manchester Central – Chinley service. The first vehicle is an LMS non-corridor wooden-bodied coach whilst the rest are LMS steel-bodied corridor coaches in the red and cream applied to main line stock at that time. ***Eric Oldham***

(Above-left) At Hague Bar the railway passes beneath a long shallow overbridge (No 16) carrying the New Mills to Marple road. The 11.45 Manchester Central – Sheffield Midland train heads towards New Mills behind Brush Type 2 No **D5841** (later Class 31 308)**.** This shallow cutting through which the train is passing is the one location where the excellent views of the Goyt Valley are temporarily hidden from view. After passing through the next overbridge (No 15 - Waterside Road), the valley once again opens up with views across to Disley and Newtown, where the LNWR Buxton Branch and MR New Mills to Heaton Mersey lines run in close proximity. **(Above-right)** Some quarter of a mile after leaving New Mills Central, BR/Sulzer Type 2 No **D5228** (later Class 25 078) heads down the 1 in 114/100 gradient towards Strines with an afternoon Sheffield Midland – Manchester Central train on 28th May 1966. To the left is an electric banner repeating signal, located some distance north of New Mills Central due to difficulty in sighting the main signals ahead, a particular condition at this location caused by the line's geographical situation. **(Below)** Running tender first light engine towards New Mills, a Class 8F 2-8-0 is passing the outer distant signal for New Mills Central. This view was taken in 1967. Hague Bar village is to the left. All(3); ***Ian R Smith***

Trains heading towards New Mills around the long sweeping curve north of the station always faced problems of visibility. The sighting of signals for Up trains took this into account with the need for an electric banner repeating signal at Hague Bar well in advance of the main signals which of necessity were located on the Down side of the line. The view to our right, taken on 31st May 1971 (***M A King***) from the north, shows a partially obscured New Mills Central, the (former) junction signal just visible above the encroaching vegetation. The quarter of a mile section on the approach to the station on 12th October 1960 was the scene of a collision between a passenger train (the 3.50pm Manchester Piccadilly to New Mills) and a freight train (the 2pm Class H Philips Park to Rowsley). It is not clear if the freight train was stationary, but the passenger train, a 6-car Derby Lightweight diesel set, ran into the rear of the goods train, the leading unit telescoping several feet in the air before coming to rest on the brake van (*see picture below*). As a result, the Driver of the DMU, Samuel Jones of Dukinfield was thrown from the cab with severe injuries. Two young children, Margaret Hibbert and Philip Whatcroft, both of New Mills, on their way home from school, became trapped in the wreckage until freed by the Fire Brigade. Driver Jones, Margaret and Philip were admitted to hospital with their injuries. Of the 43 wagons that were behind the freight engine (8F No 48443), 23 stayed on the rails. The damaged vehicles were shunted into the sidings seen in the upper picture to ascertain the extent of the damage. Diesel unit No 79170 was officially withdrawn from service in September 1961.

At New Mills station to-day the two damaged trains were shunted into this siding so that railwaymen could repair the track and clear the wreckage.

TELESCOPED!

Crash riddle of the two trains

WHILE trains crawled past the New Mills crash-spot at "caution" to-day, British Railways officials were trying to discover how two trains came to be on the same line.

The big question was: "Did the passenger train from Manchester pass a red signal; did a signalman accept two trains, going in the same direction, into his section together; or was there a technical fault in the signalling system?"

The two children hurt when the 3 50 p.m. Piccadilly - Buxton diesel ran into the back of a goods train went home from Stockport Infirmary to-day.

They were Margaret Hibbert, aged 10, of Union Road, New Mills, who was trapped for more than an hour in the wreckage, and Philip Wheatcroft, aged 12, of Low Leighton Road, New Mills, whose father saw the crash from his office across the valley.

But diesel-driver Mr. Samuel Jones, 55-year-old ex-mayor of Dukinfield, of Astley Road, Dukinfield, was "rather poorly."

Twelve-year-old Philip Whatcroft, of New Mills, who received a leg injury in the crash, was to-day said to be "comfortable."

British Railways will hold a pr[illegible]e inquiry into the crash in Manchester on Friday. Later there will be a Transport Ministry inquiry.

Wreckage was finally cleared from the tracks at 5 20 a.m. to-day. Then other railwaymen moved in to repair the track.

(Above) New Mills, c. 1920. This splendid view of New Mills, thought to be just after the Great War, shows a busy Up platform waiting the arrival of what appears to be a Hayfield branch train, although rather unusually the engine is running bunker first. The main buildings to the left, as remarked previously, have a strong resemblance to those at Marple and Hayfield. When then station buildings were cleaned in 1989, an attractive pattern of green slates was exposed on the roof and in the correct lighting conditions can still be viewed from this position. ***Courtesy W A Brown***

(Right-lower) In this view taken on 1st September 1984 from the footbridge the north-bound platform has benefitted from the provision of electric lighting. The canopy has seen its slates removed to be replaced by a felt covering and the platform has been reconstructed at a higher level. Capping of the chimneys has marginally spoilt the appearance of the main buildings but other-wise the seven decades which separate this view from that above do not reveal a great deal of change. ***T J Edgington***

(Right) New Mills Central, 1st September 1984. This view looking south from the Down platform shows Derby Lightweight (Class 108) DMU moving off to perform a movement that will allow it access to the 'siding' just inside the entrance to Hayfield Tunnel that was a remnant of the closed Hayfield branch. The former junction signal for the branch has been replaced by miniature signal arm, its purpose being to allow a train to switch from a 'running line into a loop', i.e; the siding in the tunnel. This denotes that the remaining 'stub' of the Hayfield line is by now classed as a 'loop', in this instance for holding terminating trains (such as this one) prior to their returning on the Down (northbound) line, all under the control of the one signal box. The two bridges seen here cater for the restricted nature of the site. Station Road bridge (No 14) provided the original access route. Its initial narrow construction made it difficult for both pedestrian and road users so a timber footbridge (14A) was erected in 1887 to give relief. The road bridge was subsequently reconstructed in 1908, but not before the Midland Railway had replaced the earlier footbridge in 1903 with the steel version seen here. The irony of this is that the train spent as long in the tunnel as it would have done to complete a return journey to Hayfield. Such were the economics and policies of the 1960s! *T J Edgington*

(Right-lower) From 5th January 1970 the former Woodhead line trains linking Manchester Piccadilly and Sheffield travelled via Marple and the Hope Valley, with one stop at New Mills Central. On 1st September 1984, a Class 31/4 (Brush Type 2) pulls into New Mills with the 09.15 Manchester Piccadilly – Sheffield Midland train. These trains were diverted away from this route, travelling via Stockport Edgeley in 1985 with the opening of the Hazel Grove chord linking the LNWR and Midland routes. The use of these locomotives was a reminder of the mid-1960s when they were used on some stopping trains on the route. *T J Edgington*

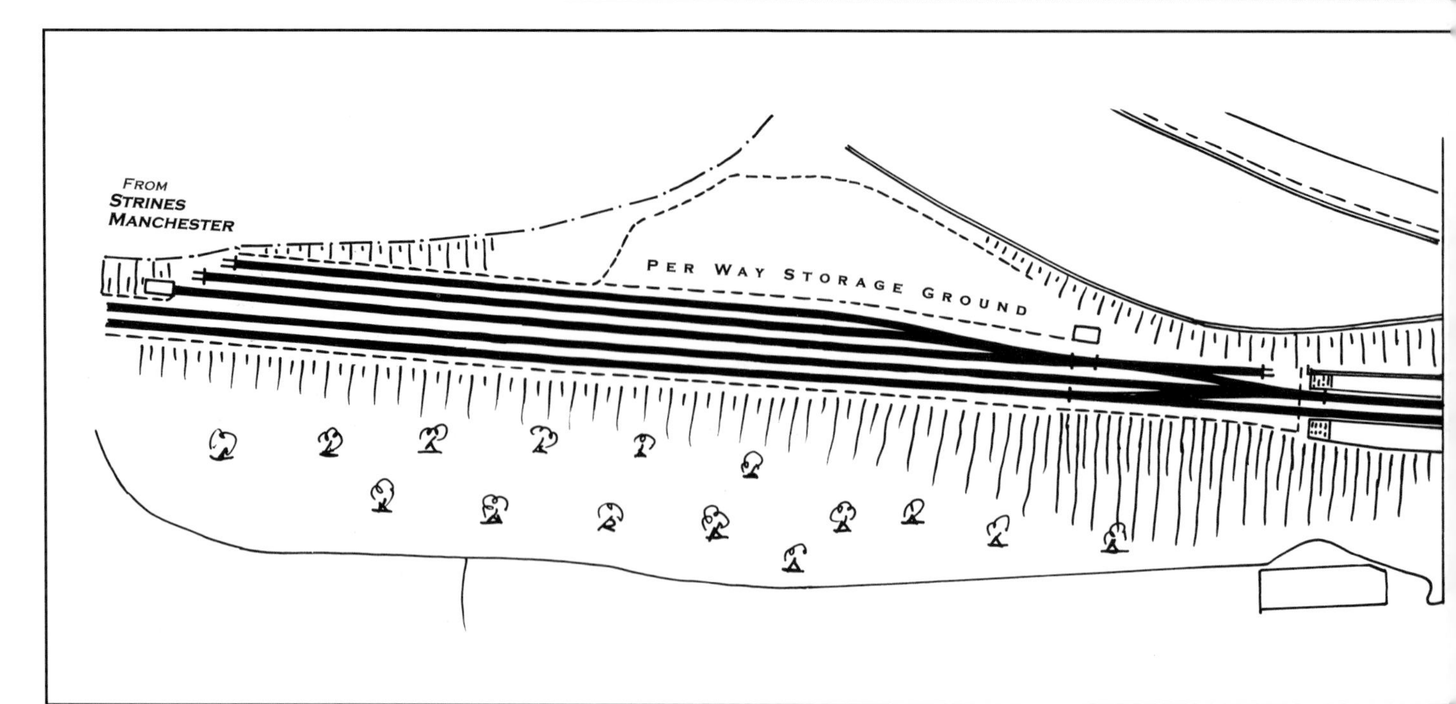

New Mills Central, c. 1958. Thompson designed Class L1 2-6-4T No **67751** pulls alongside the Up platform with a stopping train from Manchester London Road and will terminate here. These powerful engines replaced the Great Central built locomotives, latterly Class A5s and C14s, on the Hayfield and Macclesfield Central routes, 67751 being of the second batch allocated to Gorton in 1958. The Class also operated between Manchester Central and Guide Bridge with trains for the Woodhead route, being replaced by electric traction at Guide Bridge. ***W A Brown***

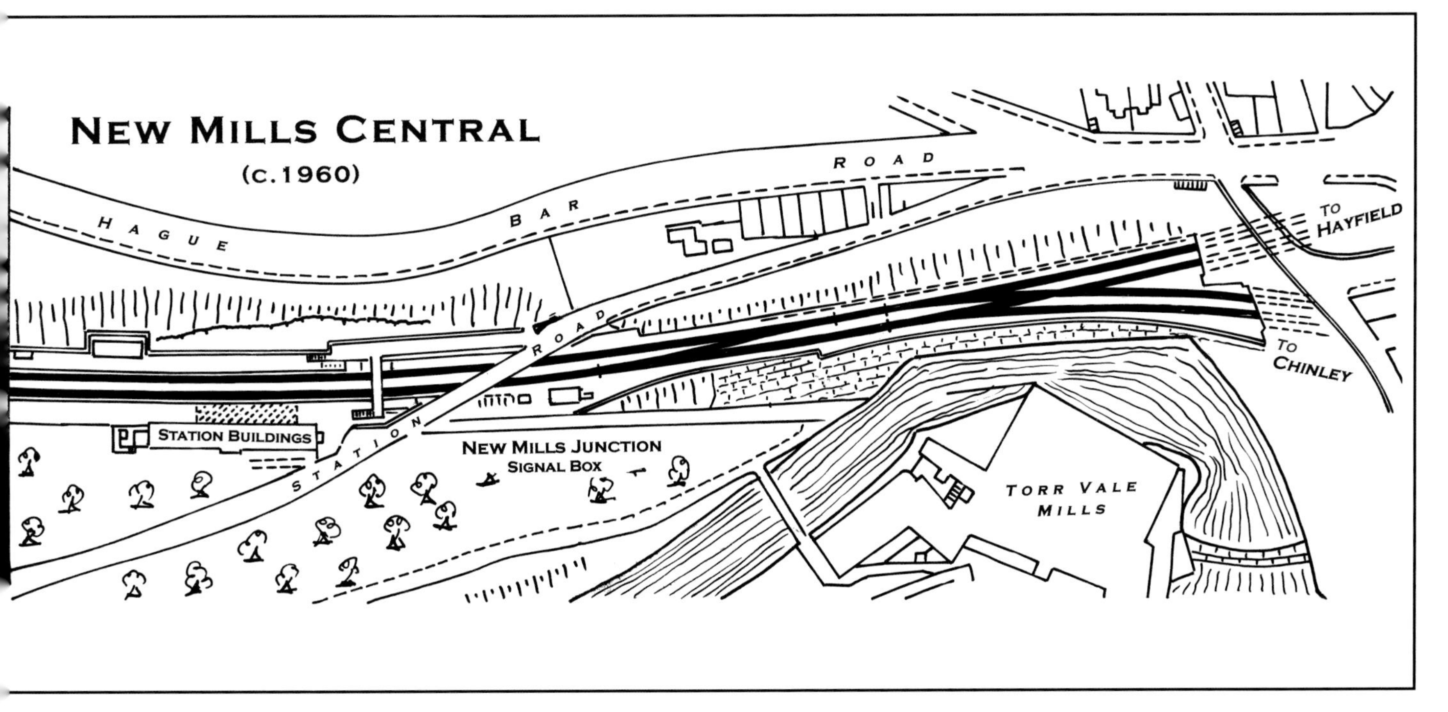

(Right) New Mills Central, c. 1958. Looking north towards Marple along the Down platform, we see once again a virtually unchanged view. Although somewhat difficult to pick out, the tall bracket signals in the distance necessitated the need for the banner repeater signal seen on page 105. The waiting shelter on the Up side was eventually replaced by the basic stone structure seen on page 108. ***Stations U K***

(Below) For a number of years following the widespread use of diesel multiple units on Hayfield line trains, one morning and one evening service remained steam hauled in order to have more seating capacity. On 21st March 1961, an unidentified LMS-built Stanier 4MT Class 2-6-4T, emerges from Hayfield Tunnel heads a rake of LMS non-corridor suburban stock out of Hayfield Tunnel and into New Mills Central Station. This was the 08.00 Hayfield – Manchester Piccadilly train and was balanced by the 17.30 from Manchester to Hayfield. By that time locomotive servicing facilities at Hayfield had ceased resulting in the need for an early morning working to Hayfield and an evening return. ***A Moyes***

(Above) This dramatic 1955 view from an elevated position on Strines Road shows LMS built Class 4F No **44114** leaving the confines of New Mills Tunnel, possibly at the head of a freight train. The relative positions of the tunnels and identifying nameboards is clearly illustrated, as is the Hayfield line signal protecting the junction. ***B Hoper***

(Right) The two tunnels at New Mills in the early 1960s. On the left is the line to Hayfield, taken beneath the town through a 197 yard long tunnel (Br No 13). On the right the Manchester Line (Old Route) arrives via New Mills South Junction through New Mills Tunnel (Br No 132 *on the Rowsley to New Mills line, the structures numbered from Ambergate*). This tunnel was 120 yards in length. A smoke-encrusted lower quadrant signal, underslung for better sighting, guards the Hayfield line. To the right but out of the picture is the retaining wall protecting the sheer drop down to the swirling waters of the River Goyt *(see page 112)*. ***D Ibbotson***

(Left-Opposite page) One of the huge engineering hurdles to be overcome when constructing the line is seen in this 1967 view of the massive retaining wall supporting the railway adjacent to New Mills Junction, a short distance south of the station. The tunnel entrance partially visible was for trains to and from the Chinley direction, whilst the bracketed signal is for trains coming off the Hayfield branch. The erosive potential of the River Goyt when in flood can easily be imagined. This magnificent structure can nowadays be viewed closely by courtesy of the unique 'Millennium Walkway', which is part of a walk around a part of the town known as the 'Torrs'. To the right of the picture is the multi-storeyed Torr Vale Mill, where towelling was manufactured until comparitively recently. ***Ian R Smith***

(Right-upper) The location of New Mills Central was physically awkward, being located on a 'shelf 'built high above the River Goyt. The steep lane serving the station can be discerned sloping away to the left - above the first two wagons of the train - with the main road from Hague Bar remaining on a horizontal plain just above. A Stanier 8F 2-8-0 No **48171** hauls a train of empty coal wagons southbound for Gowhole through New Mills Central in 1967. The tunnel entrance to the right is for the Hayfield line. This train will continue to the right of the Hayfield line tunnel almost immediately diving into a separate tunnel under the town centre of New Mills. ***Ian R Smith***

(Below) An unidentified Class B1 4-6-0 glides into New Mills Central with a train from Sheffield Midland to Manchester Central on 23rd September 1963. The tunnel mouth with the white signal post seen above the first coach is that of Hayfield tunnel on the branch. ***A Moyes***

(Right) The southern end of the Hayfield Tunnel (197 yards) in the 1960s. The area above the tunnel mouth is known as Torr Top and has for many years provided car parking facilities for the nearby shops in Market Street and Union Road, emphasising somewhat that the line has come under New Mills town centre. Viewed from the bridge parapet of Hyde Bank Road (No 11), the double line formation will continue for something like three quarters of a mile although at New Mills Tunnel End signal box a crossover creates the single line that continues right through to Hayfield. Between the tunnel and Hyde Bank Road is the culverted River Sett (No 12), although early Midland Railway engineering records would have us believe that it was the River 'Kinder'. ***D Ibbotson***

(Centre) Having cleared the tunnel, this Hayfield-bound train enters the single line section, the loco having just passed beneath Church Lane bridge (No 10). The fireman of Class C13 4-4-2T No **67412** prepares to receive the token to allow access to the single line for Hayfield on 23rd August 1952, whilst a passenger in the first carriage leans out of the window to observe the procedure. The first three coaches are of Great Central origin, whilst the last two are LNER-designed Gresley stock. The track to the right of the engine was a long siding serving the Watford Bridge Print Works, identified in the *LMS Sectional Appendix to the Working Time Tables (Midland Division) March 1937* as Messrs Rumneys Sidings. It is not totally clear when operations ceased here but there was certainly not much evidence of use from the 1950s onwards. ***N K Harrop***

New Mills Tunnel End, 12th April 1921. The signal box, a Midland Railway structure, controlled access to and from the Hayfield branch. The tablet/token was exchanged usually by the signalman standing on the landing although there were occasions when the procedure was carried out at track level. This early view shows Great Central Class 3* (Altered) 2-4-2T No **734** leaving the branch at New Mills Tunnel End on its way back to Manchester with the 1.44pm train. These engines were the mainstay of these local passenger services for almost thirty years until being replaced by the Robinson 4-4-2 tank engines. (* as LNER Class F1 No **5734,** the engine was withdrawn in September 1931). ***Courtesy W A Brown***

New Mills Tunnel End, c. 1958. The view today from the same vantage point on Church Lane bridge has changed almost beyond recognition. But in 1958, the signal box here was the point at which Hayfield branch trains handed over or collected the single line 'token' which enabled the safe journey to be made over the two miles or so of single line to the Derbyshire village. A crew member of the Hayfield bound train will be preparing to collect the 'token' from the signalman - in position at the front of the box - in order to continue along the branch. This procedure was carried out upwards of thirty times every day - if you include movements on and off the branch - including Sundays as late as 1967, the latter being something of a surprise when officialdom was looking to close the line! The buildings to the left of the line belonged to the long established engineering company of Dilworth & Morris, whilst the trough girders and decking just beyond the signal box locate the position of 'Liquer Works' bridge (No. 9) which carried the railway over an access to an adjacent one time chemical works. The line to the left of the main line was classified as a 'Lie-Bye Siding' although its main function was to service the Watford Bridge Printworks - from about 1898 - following an agreement with Rumneys, the owners. The works were taken over by the Calico Printers Association in 1930 for a different use. Between 1939-45, the Ministry of Munitions took possession of the site and it is reasonable to expect that the siding would have at least remained in use throughout the war years. Most of the site is now occupied by Leisure and Medical Centres. The Sett Valley Trail commences beyond the overbridge in the distance. Betwen ten and eleven minutes was allowed for the journey time between here and the terminus at Hayfield, allowing for the fact that this was the steepest gradient, at 1 in 78, on the branch. ***Signalling Record Society /Scrimgeour Collection***

New Mills Tunnel End, 3th January 1970. The signalman has just collected the single line token from a train leaving the branch. The photograph was taken from the second of the DMU carriage windows, just after the actual handing over process. ***G K Fox***

A cold and frosty morning, the 2rd January 1970. The last Friday in the life of the Hayfield branch. All is still as we listen for the sound of bells from the New Mills Tunnel End box, an announcement that will signal the approach of a train. Containing a 10-lever frame, the signal box had taken over responsibility for issuing/collecting the train staff from New Mills Junction in 1907. Although its prime function was to control movements on and off the branch, there was also a requirement to protect the main line when shunting operations were taking place on the siding. New Mills Tunnel End box closed on 5th January 1970. ***G K Fox***

New Mills Tunnel End, c. 1958. With a train of coal 'empties', comprising steel built 16-ton Mineral wagons, an unidentified Class J11 0-6-0 leaves the single line section of the Hayfield branch with Trip 85, on the first stage of its return journey (from Hayfield) to Godley Junction. By now operating on a Monday, Wednesday and Fridays Only basis, the loco started the turn by running light engine from Gorton shed to Godley Junction where it would pick up its train and depart at 11.58am. Arriving at Woodley at 12.10pm, thirty five minutes were allowed for shunting. A fifteen minute stop at Marple was the next target but to detach wagons only. Departing at 1.15pm, calls at New Mills Central (17 minutes) and Birch Vale (10 minutes) would follow in anticipation of spending one hour and thirteen minutes at Hayfield (arr. 2.10pm). Departing at 3.23pm, next stop was Marple where 47 minutes was allowed for shunting. Romiley (arr. 4.44pm) was allocated just eight minutes for duties before another lengthy stint at Woodley (arr. 5.2pm) of one hour and eighteen minutes all but completed the return journey. Freight duty finished on arrival at Godley Junction just after half past six. ***R Keeley***

(Left-centre) Although the maximum line speed on the branch was 35 mph, the descent towards New Mills, and in particular the Tunnel End signal box, was always approached with some caution. Passing the Highfield housing estate in the early stages of its journey to Manchester, Class C13 4-4-2T No **67423** coasts down the 1 in 78 gradient with the usual five carriages in readiness for the four miles per hour requirement to deliver the branch token to the signalman. The tidiness of the railway cannot be ignored; very little shrubbery on the embankment, a neat and tidy cess, and what appears to be spotless ballasting, recalling the days when the platelayer would sieve the ballast to keep it clear of ashes and other undesirable materials that prevented efficient drainage; circa. 1956. ***Anon***

(Left) Wild's or *'Wyldes'(sic)* Crossing, in the summer of 1963, sees the approach of a four car Derby Lightweight DMU en route for Hayfield. Drivers were expected to sound their horn on the approach to this crossing, situated at Thornsett on the New Mills side of Birch Vale. The signals 'protecting' the crossing give a very contradictory message to oncoming trains, and no doubt other users as well, but with the branch operating under the protection of a single line token, it would be the same train that returned, the signals only being placed at danger if the crossing was 'closed' to rail. Locally referred to as 'Garrison' crossing because of the nearby mill of that name, there was a small covered frame of four levers operating home and distant signals. ***G K Fox***

(Above) Birch Vale, 21st April 1956. An almost 'timeless' scene at the only intermediate station on the Hayfield branch. 'Regulatory' motive power in the hands of Class C14 4-4-2T stands alongside the platform with a Hayfield to Manchester London Road stopping train. The small goods yard is still in use, no doubt serving the needs of the nearby printworks which lay below the station to the left. The deep wrought iron girders in the foreground carried the railway over Station Road, the bridge (No 1) having the largest span of any bridge on the branch. It was built to cater for double track should the need arise. ***A C Gilbert***

(Right-centre) Birch Vale Station in 1962, looking north towards New Mills. The line changes gradient from 1 in 119 to 1 in 99 as it passes through the station. The signal, almost permanently in the 'off' position, is a Midland lower quadrant distant signal. On the left is the goods shed, of more substantial construction than the passenger station. Built of stone this shed has a through line which ends at the buffer stop to the left of the running line. ***Mowat Collection***

(Below) Five decades earlier than the view at the top of the page. No train on this occasion, but the goods yard is active. The local coal merchant was Ewart Lowe, whose family continued to run the business on the site after withdrawal of facilities in 1964. Apart from the loss of the building to the left housing the Porters Room, there is little overall change. Hudsons Soap is well represented on the advertising panels, as is Pears. Midland and Great Central poster and timetable boards occupy the same positions as those of their successors. The Midland influence can be seen in the provision of platform furniture, barrows and wall-bracket oil lamps. However, the distinctive sawn diagonal fencing would not appear for a few years. Another Midland detail, the earth-filled sleeper and rail 'buffer' is prominent at the end of the goods shed siding. Compare this with its rail-built replacement in the upper picture. Notice also the 'hyphen' between Birch and Vale. Locally however, villagers have always referred to it as 'Birch'. ***courtesy Norris Lawton***

(Right) Birch Vale, 12th March, 1966. The decline in the fortunes of the railways nationally is mirrored somewhat in this view from the now derelict site of the former goods yard as a Derby Lightweight DMU enters the station with the 11.00 ex-Manchester Piccadilly to Hayfield train via Reddish (arr. Birch Vale 11.43) A day return fare to Manchester cost the princely sum of 6/3d (32p). What an attraction this must now seem when it was possible, by catching the 08.03 (express from Marple) to be in Manchester just a half an hour later. The passenger facilities are unchanged although the platform is fully exposed to the elements following the removal of the goods shed. Withdrawal of goods facilities took place from 2nd November 1964, so the demolition men who moved in did not take long to remove traces of a once thriving, albeit small, local public facility.

A C Gilbert

(Centre) Looking towards Hayfield, this April 1962 view once again shows the minimal facilities on offer at Birch Vale. Its position on an embankment gave the station 'building' a somewhat less than permanent look compared with other stations serving the Marple to Hayfield section as first promoted.

N D Mundy

(Below) A panoramic view of Birch Vale around 1900 from the north. The terraced houses mark the route of the Hayfield to New Mills Road whilst further down the hillside, the goods shed and station take the middle ground. Whilst Birch Vale Print Works occupies the lower left of the picture, the chimney is built on the other side of the railway.

New Mills Local History Society

Birch Vale, 18th May 1957. Less than three quarters of a mile will see C14 No **67447** and its train from Manchester London Road enter the terminus at Hayfield. The engine is just about to pass the site of the signal box - closed in 1910 - that once existed at the station. It also remains unclear how often the siding in the left foreground has been used as there would appear to have been some element of land slippage. The goods yard however seems active, *Local Instructions in the Sectional Appendix to the Working Timetable* dictating that no vehicle shall be allowed to stand on the main line (during shunting operations) without an engine being at the New Mills end. This particular engine was just a month away from its fiftieth birthday and was a familiar performer on these services. It was withdrawn in December 1958. ***W Potter***

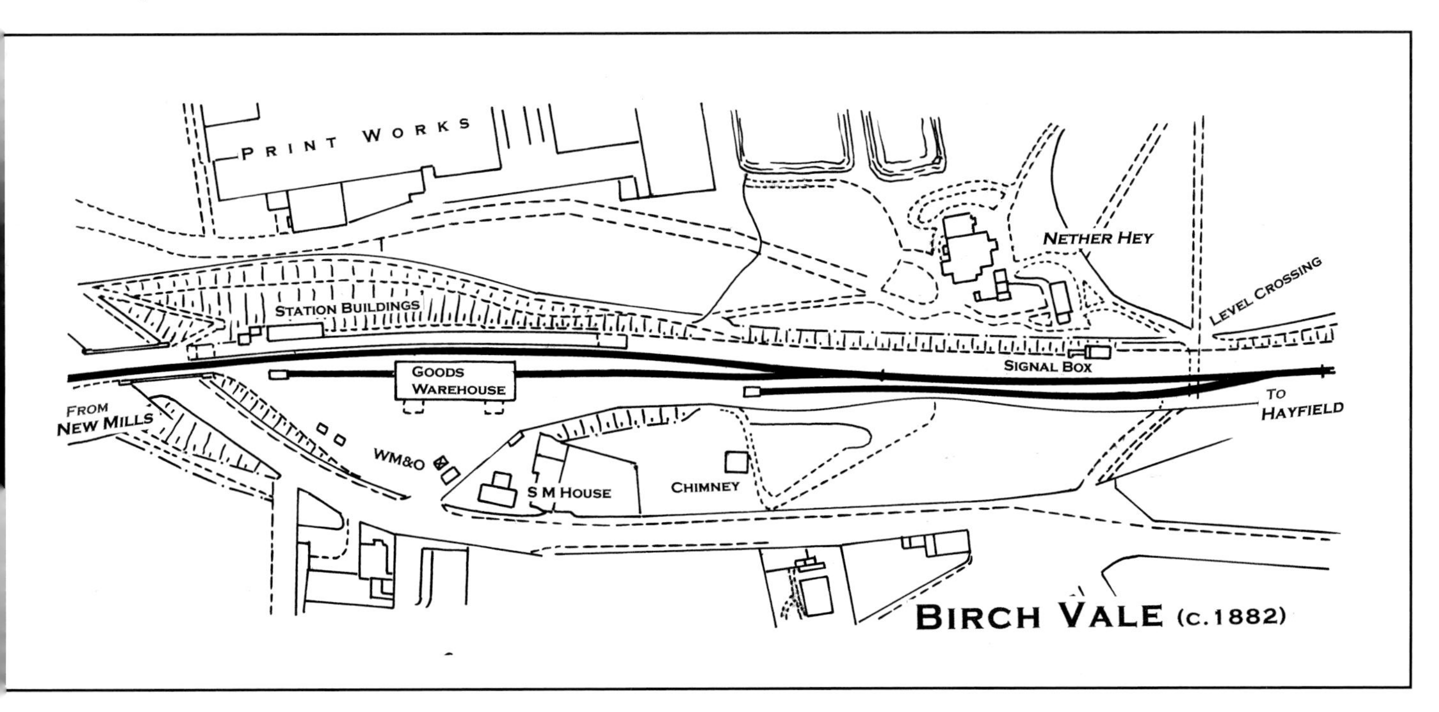

Hayfield, 9th March 1952. The last hundred or so yards on the climb into Hayfield, although still single line operation, reverted to a double track formation and a quarter of a mile ascent at 1 in 100 which ended on the station side of the signal box. Here we see C14 4-4-2T No **67451** approaching Slack's Crossing with the usual five coach train from Manchester. The Sett Valley has now opened out as the line approaches the Hayfield terminus and it is interesting to imagine what the scene might have been had the LNWR Disley and Hayfield branch, which would have been parallel to the left at this point, come to fruition. ***N R Knight***

Hayfield, c. 1956. The fireman of C14 No **67441** stoops from the footplate to hand over the single line token to the Hayfield signalman. The 'token' was part of a large hoop with leather pouch which the signalman would pass his arm through to collect as the loco passed. In this view the signalman has positioned himself to complete the procedure. The slender track crossing was illuminated from the signal box which was a Midland pattern using 'standard' components and dating from 1925 when it replaced an earlier structure located on the Hayfield side of the level crossing. The box had a twenty lever frame but its use was much reduced following withdrawal of goods facilities at the station in April 1963. Once again we see an engine in the final years of its life. In this instance, this Beyer Peacock built engine, Great Central Class 9L, saw light of day in May 1907. It was withdrawn in August 1957. ***W A Brown***

(Above) Hayfield, 26th August 1956. Class C14 (Ex-Great Central Class 9L) 4-4-2T No **67451** awaits departure time at the head of the 3.18pm Hayfield – Manchester London Road via Hyde. The carriages, all suburban non-corridor types, are *(from l to r)* a BR Mark 1; an ex-LNER Gresley wooden-bodied coach; an ex-LNER Thompson steel-bodied coach; another Gresley coach; and an ex-Great Central coach. The goods yard (left) still has business although the coal sidings are partially occupied by passenger rolling stock. On the right the locomotive shed has three engines, all of Great Central origin, occupying its single line. First is an A5 Class 4-6-2T, followed, more than likely, by a pair of C13/14 4-4-2Ts. The original wooden water tower was replaced by the 'parachute' structure seen here. **(Below)** Having moved from the station 'throat' to a point adjacent to Station Road, the photographer has recorded this view towards New Mills of the same train as above. On the left are carriages used both for strengthening trains to cater for increased numbers of passengers, as well as for stabling complete trains between turns. The use of the former Great Central carriage on the back of the train could possibly have been such a strengthening move, maybe for hikers returning after their Sunday outing on the slopes of Kinder, or the local cafe ! Both: ***T J Edgington***

A wonderful view of Hayfield, circa 1905. A seven coach train of six wheeled Manchester, Sheffield and Lincolnshire Railway built coaches is heading downhill for Birch Vale, and on to Manchester London Road. The locomotive, of MS&LR origin, in the time-honoured Hayfield line practice of travelling bunker first to Manchester, is by now GCR Class 3 2-4-2T No **574**. The MS&LR had become the Great Central Railway in 1897. On the left the goods yard is full of wagons, as are the sidings in the centre of the picture, although the positioning of the latter could have been associated with the Kinder 'Waterworks' railway that connected the station with the dam construction site some distance away. The wooden structure on the right was the water tower, used for replenishing locomotives outside the single road engine shed. This was replaced in the 1920s with a 'parachute' water crane. The small pile of stone in front of the wagons marks the site of the locomotive turntable that had at one time served the depot *(see below)*. ***courtesy John Edgington***

(Above) For those who doubt the existence of a locomotive turntable at Hayfield, here is the evidence! It has not been possible to establish an exact date when this picture was taken but the engine, a Sacre 0-6-0 No **246** of the Manchester, Sheffield and Lincolnshire Railway has been especially positioned at right angles to the running line for this portrait. Built in July 1867 by Beyer Peacock and classed as a standard goods engine, she was renumbered 321 by the Great Central in July 1904 and scrapped in October 1910. The turntable appears to be just large enough to accommodate the engine and one suspects that an increase in the sizes of a new generation of motive power saw an end to this facility. It had disappeared by the time the photograph above was taken so one can only guess at the date. However, on this occasion, No 246 appears in splendid condition and shows the livery and lines of this class of engine almost to perfection.
courtesy W A Brown

(Right) A May 1953 view of Hayfield shed with C13 No **67403** taking water prior to its working a train to Manchester (see opposite-top of page). Three engines and five crews were based at the depot with the 'home' crews working the morning trains and Gorton men in the afternoon. In LNER days, Hayfield Driver Frank Hardman recalls that several of the C13s were regularly allocated to Hayfield, but one in particular, No 5115 (1924 numbering, latterly BR No 67438), spent more time than most at the depot. ***A C Gilbert***

Hayfield, 9th March 1952. Upon arrival at Hayfield, passengers towards the rear of the trains were still left with an lengthy walk along the platform before reaching the station entrance some distance away. Having allowed its passengers to alight, the engine would then propel its carriages a short distance along the platform in order to make the short run forward again before reversing to run round the train, if necessary crossing over to the shed to take on water. Our photographer has moved quickly from Slack's Crossing *(page 120)* in time to record this procedure as C14 No **67451** reverses through the crossover to run past its train. The chimney at nearby Woods Mill is once again prominent, as is the wooden goods shed, the pattern of which was repeated at Strines, Marple and Woodley. Note also that the tail lamp has been placed on the end of the carriage. ***N R Knight***

Hayfield, 9th May 1953. Another day, another train, but having completed the same procedure as described above. This time however, the smaller of the Robinson designed 4-4-2Ts, a Class C13 No **67403**, in what appears to be ex-works condition, having taken on water and with a bunker full of coal, waits to depart with a train for Manchester. Once again, spare carriages are to be found in the sidings adjacent to Station Road and all the rails are shiny, suggesting recent activity. Built in 1903 at Gorton (GCR Class 9K), No 67403 gave fifty-five years of service before withdrawal in April 1955. ***A C Gilbert***

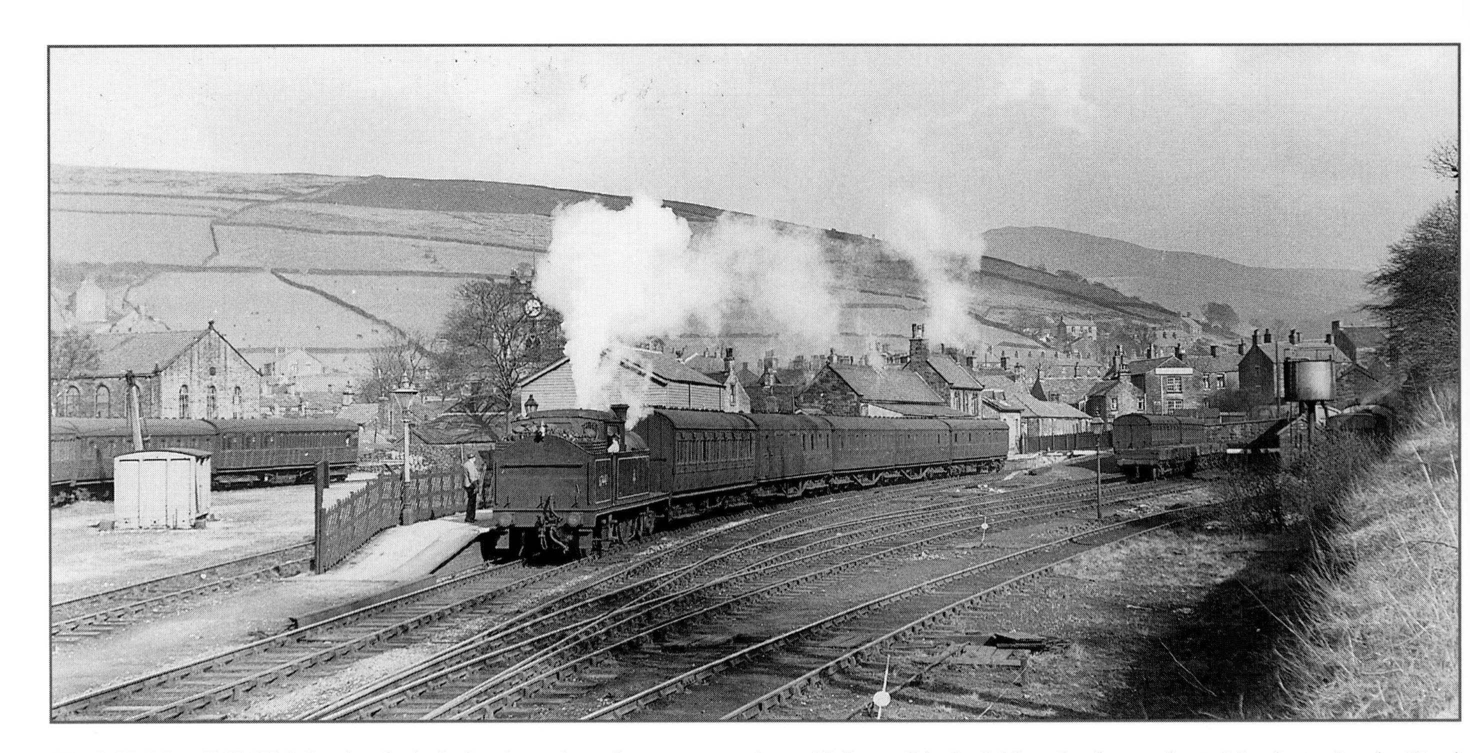

Hayfield, May 1954. With the church clock showing a time of a quarter past three, this is possibly the 3.18pm Sunday service to Manchester London Road via Hyde. The Class C14 No **67447**, with steam to spare**,** stands impatiently alongside the platform with a member of the train crew waiting in readiness for a signal from the guard to depart. Once again note the stored carriages of Great Central, LNER and British Railways origin. The train itself contains interesting examples of LNER carriages, particularly the third and fourth vehicles which comprises an articulated set. The fifty four minute journey to Manchester included stops at all but Fairfield and Ardwick stations. A note in the public timetable also indicated that a stop at Birch Vale would only be made on Good Friday, 8th April 1955, and from each Sunday from 10th April 1955. The cottages at the higher level above the rear of the train mark out the location of Kinder Road on its way to Kinder Scout.
C H A Townley

Hayfield, as we have seen, was an extremely photogenic setting. Sometime in the late 1920s, LNER Class J11 0-6-0 No **5327** (GCR Class 9J - built Gorton in 1908) occupies the 'main' line (bi-directional/Up and Down) alongside a row of stored six-wheel carriages, quite resplendent in their lined teak-finish livery. The J11 received its LNER number in April 1925, which it carried until March 1946, when it was renumbered again, becoming 4440. British Railways added the '6' late in 1948 for it to become 64440. Withdrawal took place in December 1960. The double line section seen here existed between Slacks Crossing and the signal box, a distance of some 417 yards and engines approaching Hayfield (Up direction) were required to indicate with their whistles where they wished to go. One whistle for the Main line, four for the Goods Yard, three for Wood's Siding and two for the Engine Shed. In the view here from the south side of the branch, Lantern Pike fills the left of the picture above the site of Swallow House Mills. Swallow House Lane crosses the picture above the railway, its route emphasised by the new housing development to the north west of Hayfield village.
W Potter

Hayfield, 1962. The station buildings are located at the end of a wide single platform built that would accommodate hundreds of hikers and commuters alike for over a hundred years. A two car 'Original' Derby Lightweight diesel multiple unit, still sporting 'speed whiskers', waits to return to Manchester Piccadilly. The regular interval service introduced in June 1957 with the onset of diesel train operation was now well establish, with an hourly (on the hour) service to Hayfield. The return journeys were scheduled at twelve minutes past the hour from Hayfield, mostly via Reddish, although during peak hours times varied. Note the retention of the run round facility for the remaining steam hauled trains. The sidings to the right, in which four goods brake vans are situated, served as storage for both carriages and wagons. On the right is the single road engine shed (sub-shed of Gorton), by now out of use. ***Mowat Collection***

The 12.12pm (SX) Hayfield – Manchester Piccadilly train awaits departure from Hayfield on 1st August 1963 (Thursday). During the week, this service operated via Reddish, taking forty two minutes for the all stations journey. On Saturdays, this train travelled via Hyde, a fifty minute all stations journey. On this occasion we see another of the 'Original' Derby Lightweight dmus, this time with the yellow warning panel applied, of the type that dominated the route for a decade following the introduction of diesels in 1957. The station building, constructed of stone, had its station master's house nearest the buffers alongside Station Road. The weeds of summer proliferate between the rails and the sidings still provide refuge for a number of brake vans, presumably stored as public goods services yard had been withdrawn some months earlier on 15th April 1963. ***P E Baughan***

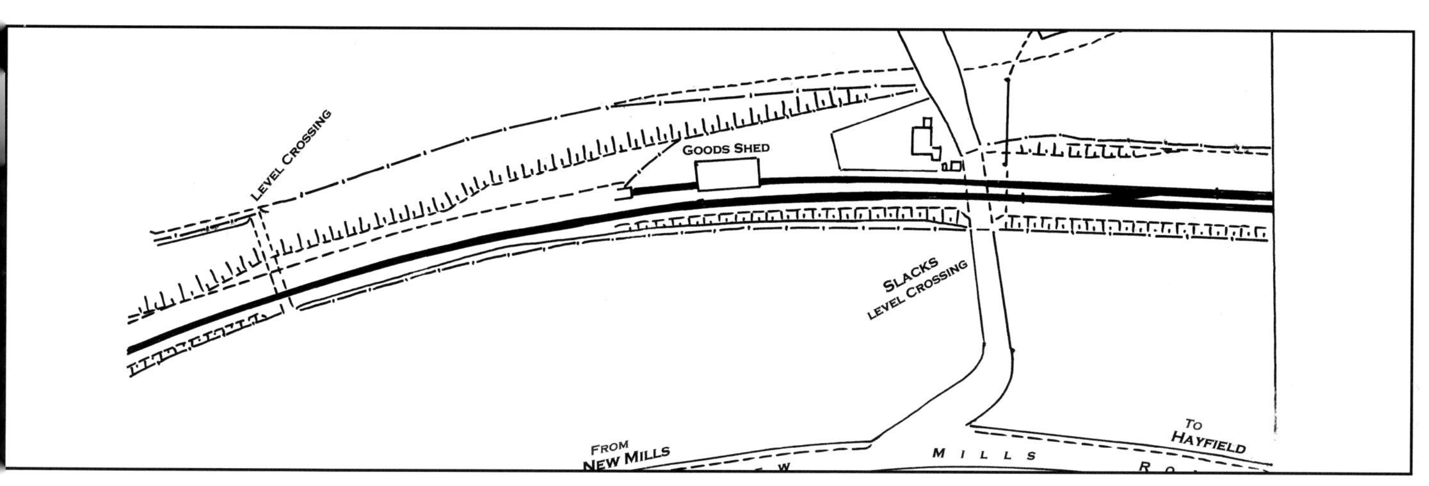

Hayfield, 18th May 1957 (Saturday). From Mondays to Fridays inclusive, Hayfield had periods of 3hrs 20mins and 1hr 58mins in the late morning and early afternoon respectively without a train from Manchester. The matter was rectified on Saturdays by the inclusion of the 10.50am and the 1.5pm services. Having completed its journey, Class C14 No **67445** positions its carriages prior to running towards the buffer stops before reversing to run round its train. One month later, the new diesel service would be introduced, together with the regular interval operation that would transform travel opportunities on the branch. A Second Class cheap day return fare of 3/2d (16p) between Manchester and Hayfield was available, First Class 50% more. The nameboard on the wall of the goods shed has been removed and replaced by a maroon enamel sign at the New Mills end of the platform. ***W Potter***

Hayfield Station in 1962. A four car Derby Lightweight dmu arrives with a train from Manchester Piccadilly. The goods yard has entered its last year of operation and the sidings in the foreground are by now seeing only limited use. Note the freshly ballasted track to the left of the diesel, still needed for the steam operated services. ***J. Spencer Gilks***

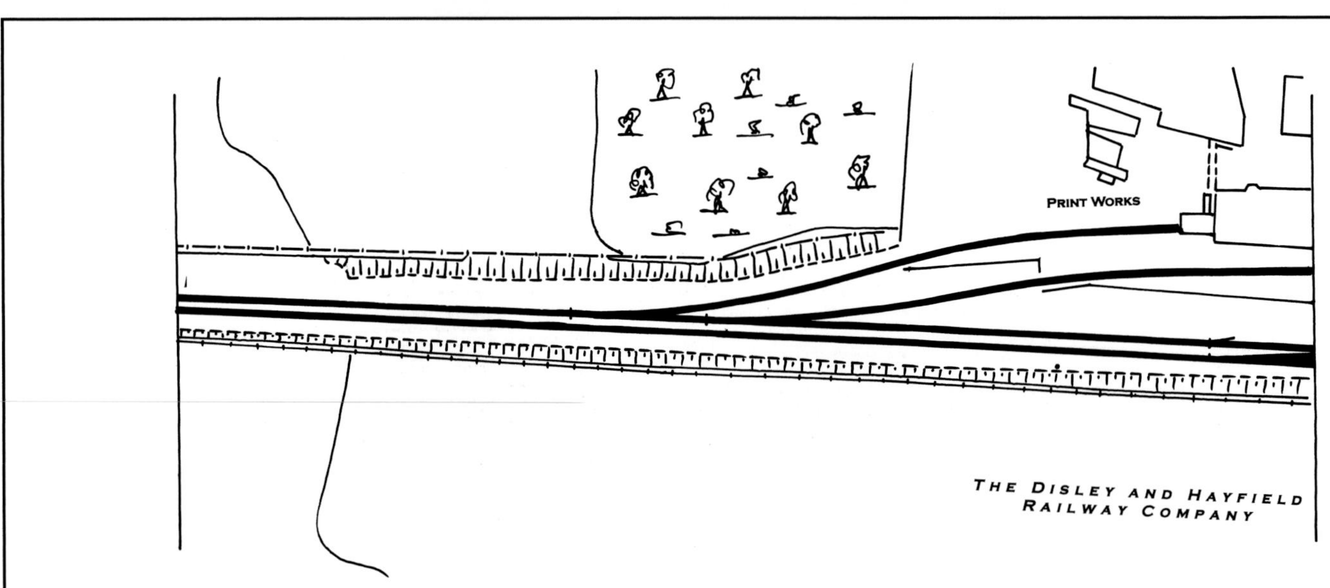

HAYFIELD

Hayfield, 2nd August 1969. Passengers sit in the shade of the station canopy during the last summer of operation on the branch. The station buildings that have served Hayfield for over a century will close for business in just over four months time, the decision taken to withdraw train services from the branch being displayed on the notice boards further along the platform (see picture to the right). The rugged stone-built features of the station were replicated in the buildings at New Mills and Marple, particularly the attractive arched windows and doorway of the Station Master's House at the far end of the platform. **(Right)** The ticket 'barriers' that latterly were anything but, most passengers walking around them. One notice declares the intentions of the British Railways Board, to close the line, whilst another details 'alterations' to services. Finally, the Area Manager, a Mr A Stonehewer, offers to 'solve your travel problems' - by closing the railway ?

M A King

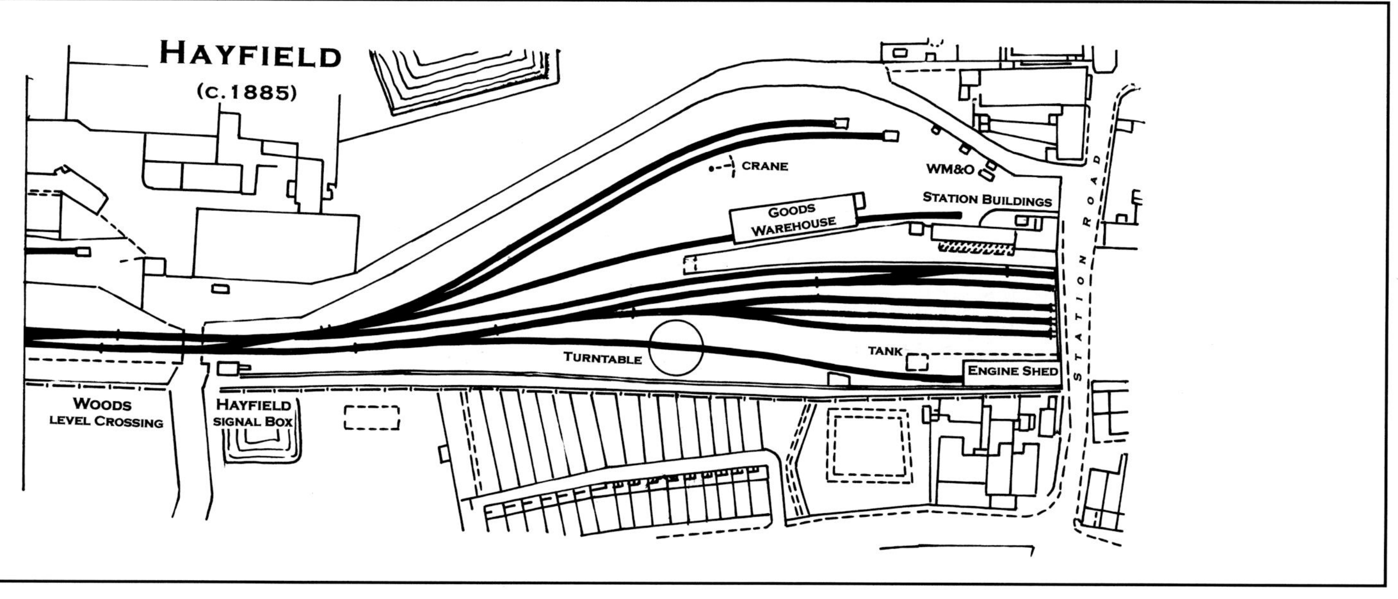

HAYFIELD

THE END OF THE LINE.

(Right) British Railways Class C13 No **67423** rests at the end of its journey from Manchester, one of the many countless times it has made the trip. For nearly twenty years, these Great Central built engines all but monopolised the eastern suburban services out of London Road. This Robinson designed locomotive had left Gorton Works new in October 1904 and would be withdrawn in October 1957, fifty three years after entering service. This Friday evening scene at the terminus of the branch from New Mills, 28th February 1953, will evoke the many memories we have of the 'Hayfield line' and the service it provided for over a century.

E R Morten

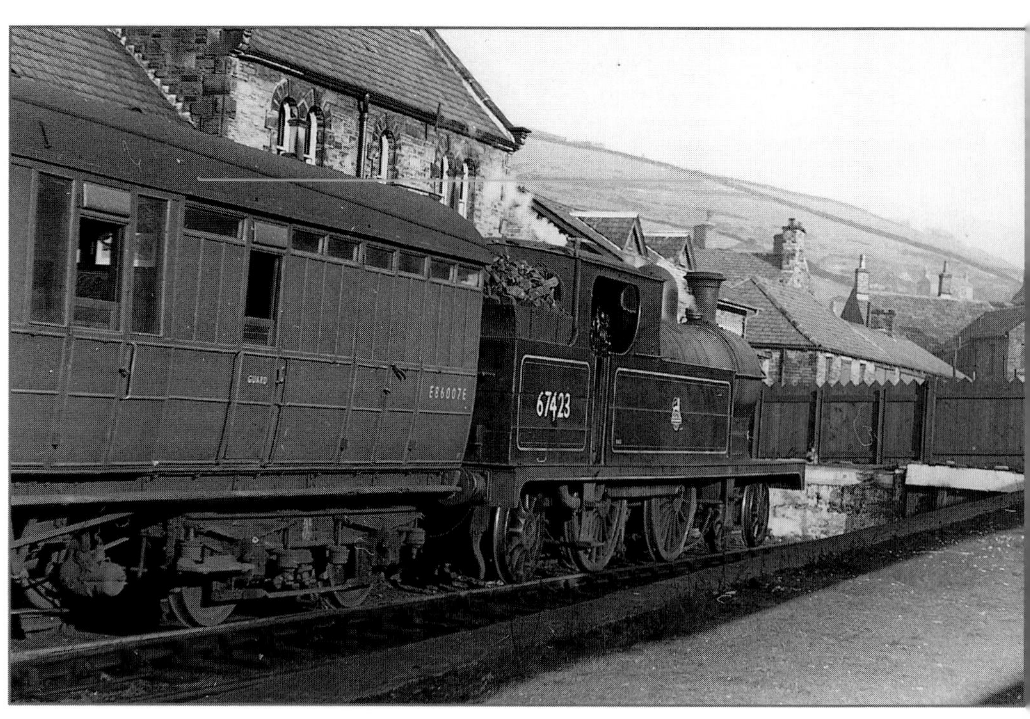

Hayfield, 2nd August 1969. A view of station buildings from Station Road. The arched window detail is repeated again on the rear and side elevations. The entrance to the goods yard was over a cobbled roadway to the right of the picture. Similar notices to those on the platform are repeated overlooking Station Road for public viewing. Whilst all concerned bemoan the loss of the branch line, a piece of Hayfield lives on at the Brookside Garden Centre, Poynton, where the British Railways maroon enamel sign, seen here high up on the gable wall, is preserved for posterity.

M A King

'Vintage' HAYFIELD

Eight decades have now passed since the scenes on this page were recorded. The arrival and subsequeant operations prior to departure for Manchester made this an everyday occurrance for this engine and its crew. The view to the right shows Great Gentral Class 3 (altered) 2-4-2T No **735** adjacent to Wood's Crossing (and the signal box), on the point of returning to the station in order to rejoin its waiting train (see below - centre). In the distance is the goods shed located just beyond Slacks Crossing, some 417 yards away. Built by Neilson & Co. No **735** was one of twelve engines that appeared in 1892 with larger bunkers than earlier members of the class. A Belpaire boiler, believed to be second-hand from a Class 9G, was fitted in May 1909, 735 being the first of the class so modified. In 1923, the LNER reclassified the group of engines as F1/2. As a result of the 1924 renumbering, 735 became 5735. In 1927, further modification resulted in reclassification to F1/3. The engine was withdrawn in July 1933, three years after becoming Class F1/4.

(Centre) With bunker well-coaled, **735** awaits departure time with a nine coach train of MS&L built six-wheelers, the vehicles having reverted to the teak finish livery originally carried. Just visible by the rear of the train is the inclined ramp carrying the track that formerly provided an end-on junction with the Kinder (waterworks) railway.
courtesy J M Bentley

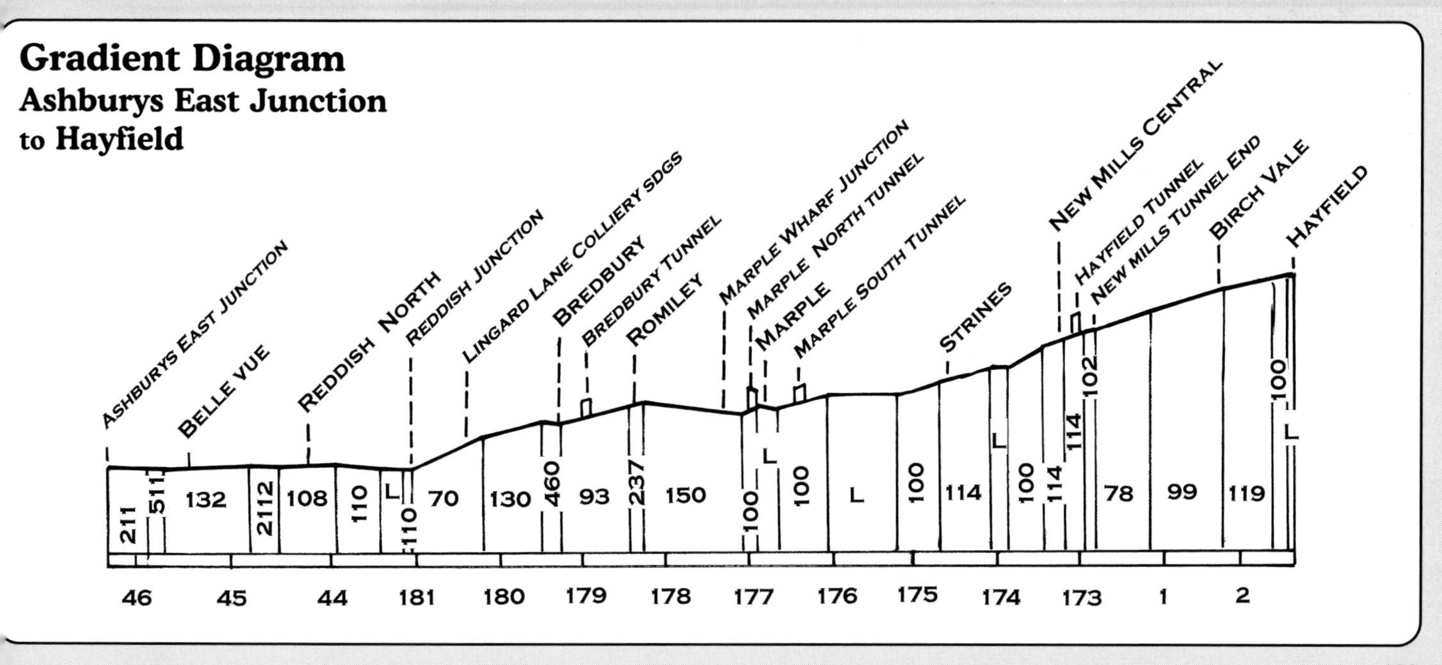

(Right) Hayfield, c.1924/25. For almost fifty years, the Midland Railway had maintained the 'infrastructure' of the joint lines, which included of course the Hayfield branch. Local responsibility came under the control of Ambergate District (later Derby North), an area organisation which broadly speaking, included the lines between Derby and Manchester. Periodic inspections of the system were carried out by Officers of the company which resulted in the occasional visit to 'outposts' such as Hayfield. Here, a Johnson 'Single' of Midland origin, now in LMS 'red' livery, rests in the (Loop) siding adjacent to the platform road after bringing an Inspection Saloon up the branch. Built sometime between 1891 and 1893 as an 1853 Class engine, (No 97), **644** had carried the number since 1907. The coal wagons to the left are prominent of course but note also the inclined ramp which, as mentioned previously, had been provided to enable a rail connection across Station Road with the Kinder (waterworks) railway. Both; ***courtesy J M Bentley***

(Centre) Locomotives in the process of going through the workshops at Gorton were frequently to be found 'running-in' following repairs/overhaul on the joint lines to the south-east of Manchester. Over the years, Hayfield had its fair share of 'visitors', this Great Central 4-4-0 Class 11B No **1019** being just one during the early days of the LNER. Pictures seen earlier in the book depicted such workings at Romiley and it is thought that the locomotive seen here will shortly couple up to a passenger train prior to a tender first return journey to Manchester. The class was first introduced in 1902, being built for the GC by Sharp Stewart & Co. The LNER reclassified the engines as D9, allocating the number 6019 in 1925. Having survived forty-six years in private ownership, some twenty-six members of the class were taken into British Railways stock in 1948. Although allocated 62306, the number was never actually carried by the time the engine was withdrawn in January 1949.

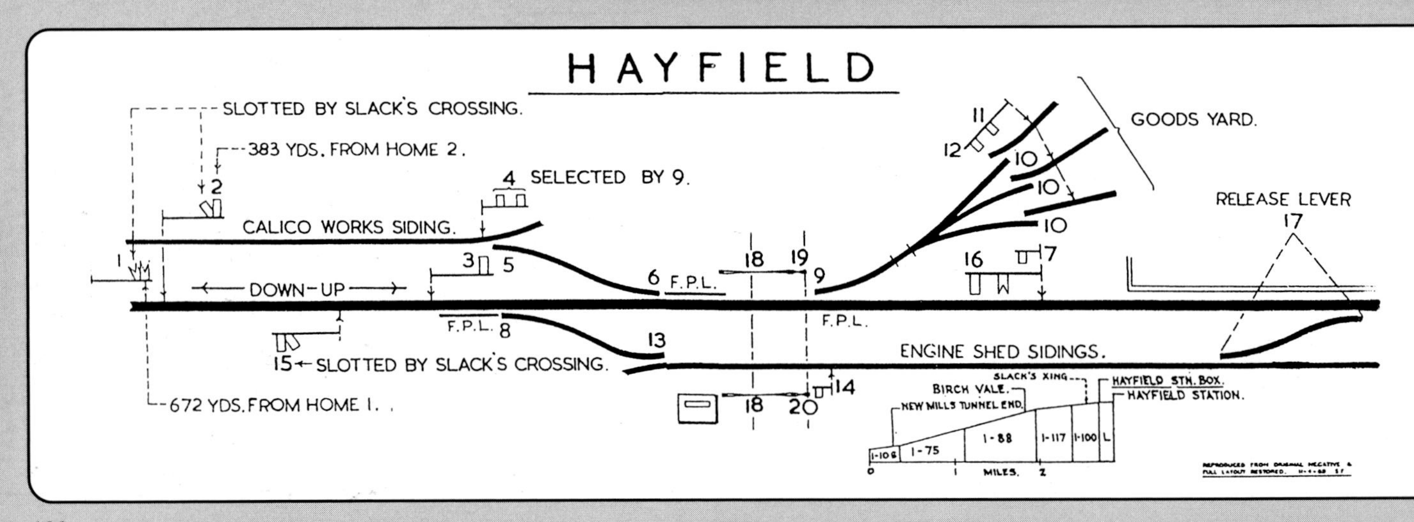

New Mills Tunnel End 'snapshots'

)ne time New Mills resident ***Melvyn Green***, ow living in Blandford Forum, Dorset, sent long a series of box camera 'snapshots', which e had taken from Hyde Bank Road and Church ane bridges at various times during 1957.

Above) An unidentified Fowler 2-6-4 tank engine autiously approaches Tunnel End signal box with a Ianchester bound train, crew member and signalman reparing for the token exchange. Summer 1957.

BETWEEN NEW MILLS JUNCTION AND HAYFIELD.

Referring to Rule 179 in the Book of Rules and Regulations, the empty carriages forming passenger trains terminating at New Mills may, when necessary, be propelled from New Mills Junction over the up main line to the dead-end siding at New Mills Tunnel End signal box, providing the continuous brake is properly connected and available for use, and a guard or shunter is in the brake van farthest from the engine. At night and during fog or falling snow, a white light must be placed on the front of the leading vehicle.

When vehicles are removed from the siding they must be drawn on to the up main line outside the up home signal in accordance with the Block Telegraph Regulations, and set back on the single line towards Hayfield, and the train must then proceed to New Mills Junction on the proper line, but the single line must not be fouled unless the driver is in possession of a train tablet.

'Drivers of freight trains and light engines may, when authorised by the signalman at New Mills Tunnel End box, return from Rumney's sidings to New Mills Tunnel End box, and drivers of freight trains and light engines may, when authorised by the signalman at Hayfield, return from Birch Vale to Hayfield, as provided in the Electric Train Tablet Block Regulations for the working of ballast trains, without going through the whole section.

Messrs. Rumney's Sidings:—

The rear portion of all trains going towards Hayfield which have to attach or detach wagons at Messrs. Rumney's sidings, must be placed in the siding provided for the purpose before shunting operations are commenced, and the points in the main line must remain open for the siding during the time such trains are attaching or detaching traffic.

Trains proceeding towards New Mills which have to attach or detach wagons at Messrs. Rumney's sidings must be brought to a stand on the Hayfield side of the connection with the sidings, and properly secured before shunting operations are commenced.

A competent man from New Mills or Hayfield must be in attendance at the siding to assist with each train stopping for traffic purposes, the Station Masters at New Mills and Hayfield to arrange accordingly.

HAYFIELD.

No vehicle or vehicles must be allowed to stand upon the main line at Hayfield unless there is on engine at the New Mills end of such vehicle or vehicles.

BETWEEN HAYFIELD AND BIRCH VALE.

A goods brake (in which a guard must ride) may be propelled in front of the engine from Hayfield to Birch Vale Station when goods and coal traffic is being worked between these points, and the brake must be secured on the main single line in Birch Vale Station whilst the empty wagons are being shunted out of the sidings to make room for the loaded traffic.

It will not be necessary in these circumstances for a brake to be in the rear from Hayfield, b' : on returning from Birch Vale to Hayfield a brake must always be in the rear.

(Left) Class J11 No **64349** leaves Hayfield Tunnel with a Hayfield bound goods 'train' of one coal wagon and brake van. Summer 1957.

(Right) Summer 1957. One of the new 'original' Derby Lightweight diesel multiple units, just introduced on the Hayfield and Macclesfield line services, leaves Hayfield Tunnel and will now slow down in readiness for the driver to collect the single line token for the branch.

(Left-lower) Class 04/7 2-8-0 No **63582** waits patiently astride the junction opposite New Mills Tunnel end signal box with an engineers train. The crossover was being replaced and advantage taken of the rarely used siding to store wagons. Occasionally, the siding was also called upon to store stock of Belle Vue excursion trains. Winter 1957.

(Right-lower) Sharing duties on the Hayfield branch with the former GC and LNER type locomotives was this Fowler 2-6-4 tank, seen here leaving Hayfield Tunnel. Summer 1957.

The Kinder Railway was a comparatively short lived undertaking built to service the building of the Kinder Reservoir two miles to the north-west of Hayfield. Under the auspices of Stockport Corporation, work had commenced in 1903. It was 1908 however before an agreement with the Great Central & Midland Joint Commitee was reached to enable the 'tramroad', as the system was described, access to the standard gauge at Hayfield station. First movements of locomotives and rolling stock across Station Road to a yard behind the George Hotel were by means of a temporary track. Early in 1909, a steeply inclined ramp, immediately south of the platform and run-round loop in Hayfield station, was brought into use to enable what would ultimately be a permanent, albeit short-lived, level crossing across Station Road. A time of approximately one hour was allowed each day for traffic to cross the road, initially for access to the yard behind the George Hotel. It is not clear when the arrangement ended but despite inaugauration of the Kinder project in July 1912, a short section at the western end of the railway, between Hayfield and the Cuckoos Nest Quarry, continued in use until 1914 for road-stone and ballast extraction.

(Above) This Hudswell Clarke 0-6-0 saddle tank had arrived at Hayfield from the makers in Leed in March 1908 and was soon at work on the two mile long system. The effect of the undertakin being classified as a 'tramway' can be seen here with no protection from the passing train afforde to either rail or road. This view north along Church Street soon after delivery of the locomotiv shows Stockport Corporation locomotive No **2** shortly after leaving the transshipment yard at th rear of the George Hotel. The area, to the east of Station Road, was used for the loading and unload-ing of materials between the 'main' line and the tramway during construction of the reservoir. Onc across the road, a bridge over the River Sett carried the line onto a route arcing the northern side o Hayfield cricket ground. The engine worked the line for over 2½ years before being sold on

courtesy W A Brown

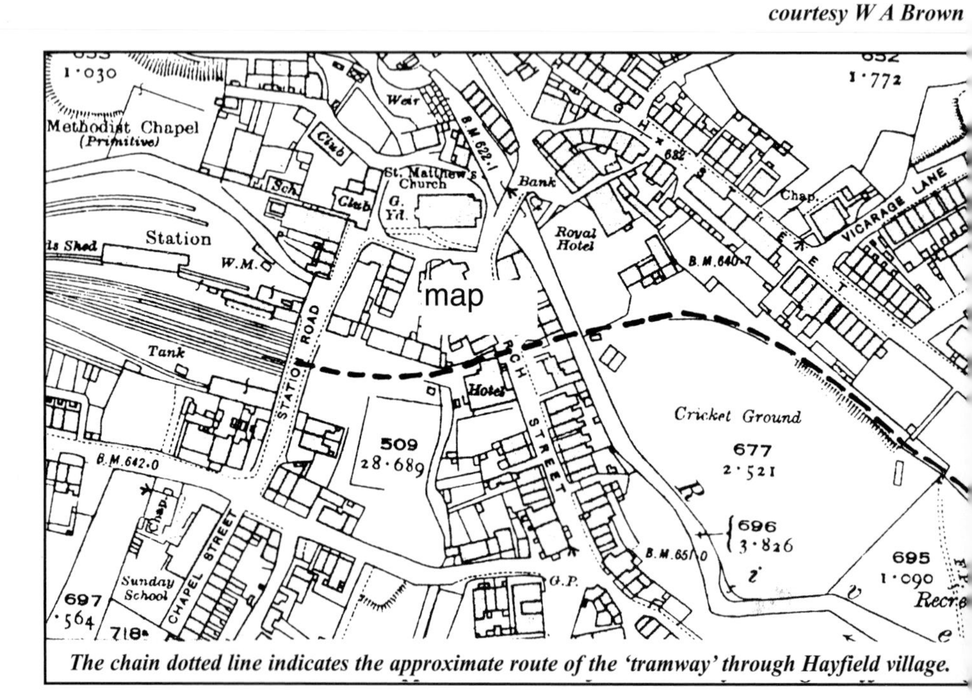

The chain dotted line indicates the approximate route of the 'tramway' through Hayfield village.

The Kinder Railway

(Right) A specially arranged photograph of Stockport Corporation locomotive No **6**, believed to be in the vicinity of Bowdens Bridge, shows an immaculately maintained 0-6-0 Saddle tank purchased from Hudswell Clarke of Leeds towards the end of 1909. All but one of the locomotives (No 7; *Moscotte,* built by Manning Wardle), were built by the Leeds company.

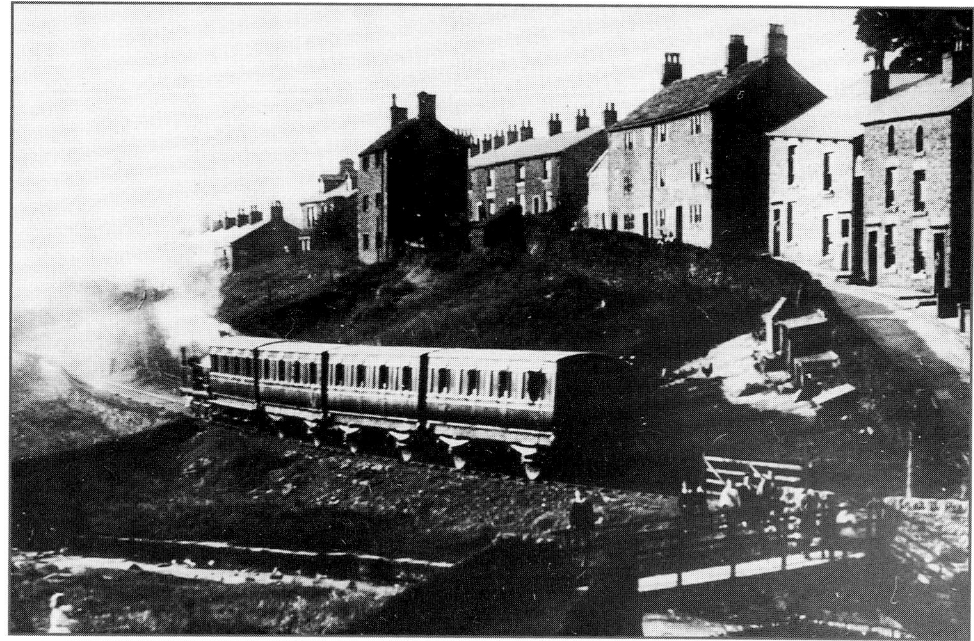

(Centre) Another well known view showing one of the Hudswell Clarke saddle tanks heading bunker first with a workmens train, popularly known as the 'Paddy' or 'Kinder' Mail, on the approach to Hayfield. The terraced houses stand either side of High Street/Kinder Road.

(Below) Unfortunately, the posed workforce made identification of the locomotive difficult, although only Nos 1 and 2 had the oblong makers plate (cabside). The well-filled train of 'navvies' is about to depart for Hayfield from the site adjacent to the reservoir works. The four carriages, acquired from the Mersey Railway, arrived at Hayfield in May 1908, a temporary track being laid across Station Road to enable the vehicles to be transferred.

A 'Last-minute' Miscellany

There is a well-known frustration amongst writers and publishers that many photographs 'turn up' when projects have either been completed or are well advanced. This book has been no exception although with a small amount of space available it was decided to have a brief reprise of some of the locations seen earlier on the routes between Manchester and Hayfield.

(Right-upper) The view of **Ardwick** shows the railway a decade on after electrification as part of the Manchester, Sheffield and Wath scheme and subsequent interface with the MLE covering the Crewe to Manchester lines. Much of the 'old' railway remained, Ardwick No 1 signal box being the prime example. Improvements at Ardwick did not however include raising the Up platform, which forever remained an obstacle to passengers. The 1988 remodelling scheme removed any necessity for this work as services were concentrated on the island platform which formerly served the Down side only. The raised footbridge produces an effective frame around one of the Derby Lightweight units about to embark on the last leg of its journey into Piccadilly. The lines immediately in front of the the signal box served the Down or West Loop together with a connection to the 'Kobo' coal sidings at Ardwick. For those with an interest with football matters, there was a link from the siding into the Hyde Road ground of Manchester City before their move to Maine Road in 1923. ***Anon***

(Centre/Lower) Ashburys, 23rd August 1970. One of the the last of the large marshalling facilities in the Manchester area in a form that had survived almost in original form. The centre view shows the approach from Ardwick. It was still a very busy piece of railway with regular passenger workings serving the eastern suburbs and vying for track occupation with an intensive freight operation. Ashburys West, located immediately beyond the platform ends, was the point at which traffic emanated from a host of locations; Ardwick Sidings and Coal Drops, Ardwick West Goods Yard, Ancoats Branch and Ashton Road, not forgetting trains traversing the Ancoats Junction line via Midland Junction from Philips Park and beyond. The open and windswept island platform here was for the brave, affording little protection from the elements. The lower view from the Down platform looking east, shows Ashburys Sidings in the distance beyond Ashburys East signal box. The connection between the goods and main lines is to the fore of the box. ***M A King***

Right) A reminder of the past at Bredbury in 955, some seven years after Britsh Railways ad taken over control of matters. The Station Aaster's House is now in private hands.

Below-centre) Woodley Junction viewed rom an elevated position on Station Road. he route to Romiley and Marple leaves on ne left of the picture, whilst that to Stockport, ne Cheshire Lines, curves away to the right eyond the goods yard. Both; ***Norman Jones***

Right) Excursion traffic in the 1950s and arly '60s was still very popular with owns and villages along the routes adiating from Manchester. The resorts of Blackpool, Southport, New Brighton were but three of the numerous 'haunts' or day trippers, particularly the spring olidays of Easter and Whit. Outings to Blackpool had a habit of starting from Buxton with LM engines and stock and erved the stations between Chinley and Belle Vue. From Hayfield, most trips were provided under Eastern Region urisdiction, in line with ordinary assenger services. This May 1961 view hows Class B1 4-6-0 No **61011,** *Vaterbuck,* during the first of its two short pells at Gorton (9G), crossing Marple Viaduct with a Hayfield to Southport xcursion. After a relatively short life of ourteen years, *Waterbuck* was withdrawn n December 1962. ***John Oldham***

BUILT 5/1929. W/DRAWN 7/1962. ASTON 1933, 1948, NUNEATON 1960.

(Right) Monday evening at **Marple** on 7th August 1961 shows 'Crab' 2-6-0 No **42811** piloting an unidentified Stanier Class Five on the 4.35pm Manchester Central to Derby train. Alongside is the 4.58pm(SX) New Mills to Manchester Piccadilly via Reddish working in the hands of one of the Derby Lightweight sets. The Derby train had run non-stop to Stockport Tiviot Dale but would then be required to provide an all stations service (Strines excepted) through the Peak District, with a connection at Millers Dale for Buxton. The 'Crab' at the time was based at Nuneaton (2B) although it had spent lengthy spells previously at Crewe(S) and Stoke.

(Centre) The rural tranquility is temporarily shattered on Friday 17th May 1963 as Class B1 4-6-0 passes **Wilds Crossing** - between Birch Vale and New Mills - on its way to Manchester with one of the few remaining steam operated services.

(Right) Birch Vale, 16th June 1961. Even a bunker first view of the L1's gave yet another impression of the power of the class. Having worked empty stock from the sidings at Hayfield, the 6.33pm Birch Vale to Manchester Piccadilly via Hyde train stands by the platform awaiting departure. Some ten minutes later, another service via Hyde would follow but this time running non-stop from Guide Bridge.

This page: ***John Oldham***(3)

THE TIMETABLE CONFIRMS THIS, BUT TWO TRAINS VIA WOODLEY & HYDE WITHIN 10 MINUTES SEEMS ODD INDEED.